The
Adobe Photoshop 2025
User Guide

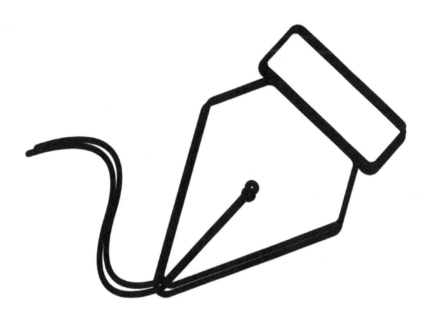

Tips and Tricks for Maximizing Performance, Productivity, and Unlocking Your Creative Potential

Ray V. Lopez

Contents

Introduction

Welcome to the World of Adobe Photoshop

As of 2025, Adobe Photoshop continues to be the preeminent software for digital imaging. Since its establishment in 1987, Photoshop has transformed the manipulation of photographs, graphics, and art. Photoshop has transformed from basic photo modifications to complex digital artwork, becoming a formidable instrument that enables professionals, artists, designers, and enthusiasts. The release of Adobe Photoshop 2025 provides users with an enhanced array of capabilities aimed at optimizing processes, fostering creativity, and advancing digital artistry.

Adobe Photoshop 2025 advances its legacy by incorporating state-of-the-art technology, artificial intelligence (AI) advancements, and accelerated processing capabilities, while preserving the fundamental tools that render it a preferred choice among creatives. The newly introduced AI-driven functionalities, such as enhanced Content-Aware Fill and Neural Filters, offer a degree of automation and accuracy that was unattainable even a few years prior. These innovations, together with the software's current suite of capabilities for image editing, illustration, graphic design, and digital painting, render it essential for any creative professional's toolkit.

Additionally, Photoshop 2025 presents performance enhancements that markedly diminish lag and enhance speed, especially when handling substantial files or intricate compositions. As creatives push the boundaries of their work with increasingly sophisticated designs and 3D features, Photoshop has developed to meet their needs without compromising on performance. Whether you're building a website layout, retouching a portrait, or producing a 3D model, Photoshop 2025's advancements ensure that your workflow remains seamless and efficient.

In this book, we will lead you through every feature and operation of Photoshop 2025, from the most fundamental tools to the more advanced approaches. This guide will assist both novices and seasoned Photoshop users in maximizing the software's capabilities.

Whom This Guide Is For

This handbook is meant for a wide variety of users. It is aimed to help both novices who have never used Photoshop before and advanced users who are wanting to improve their existing skills or acquire new techniques in Photoshop 2025. If you've never used Photoshop, don't worry; we'll take you through each tool, feature, and workflow step by step. If you're an experienced user, we'll go deep into new features and advanced approaches, helping you refine your art and enhance your efficiency.

For newbies, Photoshop can appear daunting at first. With so many tools, options, and settings accessible, it can be tough to know where to start. This guide will break everything down into easy-to-follow sections, ensuring that each topic is handled in a clear and basic manner. We'll help you get comfortable with the interface, educate you how to use the essential tools, and show you how to apply those skills in real-world projects.

For expert users, this guide will provide insights on Photoshop 2025's latest features and advancements. We'll show you how to include AI tools into your workflow, improve your picture retouching and compositing skills, and master complex tasks like digital painting and 3D design. You'll also find innovative, efficient techniques to speed up your workflow and enhance your productivity.

Ultimately, this guide is designed to be a beneficial resource for anyone trying to develop their Photoshop skills—whether you're a hobbyist, professional photographer, graphic designer, illustrator, or web designer. The tools and approaches we explore will help you enhance your workflow and unleash your creative potential.

How to Use This Guide

This book is built to accommodate both beginners and experienced users, guaranteeing that you may jump in at any time depending on your existing knowledge level. The content is structured into chapters that study various features, tools, and approaches in Photoshop 2025, each one building on the last to give a holistic learning experience. Here's how you can make the most out of this guide:

1. **Start with the Basics**
   If you're new to Photoshop, begin with the **beginner-friendly chapters** in the early part of the book. These chapters will introduce you to the Photoshop workspace, the basic tools, and essential techniques like working with layers, selections, and brushes. As a beginner, it's important to establish a solid understanding of these core concepts before moving on to more advanced topics.

2. **Jump to Advanced Features**
   If you're already familiar with Photoshop and want to dive deeper into the new features of Photoshop 2025, you can jump ahead to the chapters focusing on AI tools, 3D design, or advanced retouching. These chapters offer specialized knowledge and professional tips to help you stay ahead of the curve.

3. **Follow the Projects**

   Each chapter includes **hands-on projects** designed to help you apply what you've learned. These projects range from simple photo edits to complex designs and illustrations. Following these practical exercises will not only reinforce your understanding of the concepts but also build your confidence as you see your skills improve. The projects are structured in a step-by-step format to ensure you can follow along, even if you're not yet an expert.

4. **Utilize the Resources**

   At the end of the guide, you'll find a comprehensive **index**, a **glossary of terms**, and a section dedicated to **keyboard shortcuts**. These resources are designed to help you quickly reference anything you need while using Photoshop 2025. The **keyboard shortcuts** will be especially helpful as you progress, allowing you to work more efficiently.

5. **Refer Back When Needed**

   As you continue to use Photoshop, feel free to revisit chapters or sections that you may need a refresher on. This guide isn't meant to be read once and forgotten—think of it as a **comprehensive reference manual** you can refer back to whenever you need. Whether you're looking for a specific tool or technique, the detailed explanations and illustrations will always be at your disposal.

Getting Started with Photoshop 2025

Before you dive into the deep end of Photoshop 2025, it's important to get your setup right. Below are some simple steps to help you get started:

1. **Installation and Setup**

   To begin, download and install Photoshop 2025 from the Adobe website or through Adobe Creative Cloud. Once installed, you'll need to sign in with your Adobe ID (or create one if you don't already have one). After signing in, you can activate Photoshop and begin customizing it for your needs.

2. **Setting Up Your Workspace**

   When you first open Photoshop 2025, you'll be presented with the default workspace. However, Photoshop allows you to customize your workspace layout to suit your preferences. You can organize the panels, tools, and menus in a way that makes the most sense for your workflow. You can also save multiple workspace layouts for different tasks, such as photo editing, web design, or illustration.

3. **Understanding the Photoshop Interface**

   Upon starting Photoshop, take some time to familiarize yourself with the **Photoshop interface**. On the left, you'll find the **Tools Panel**, which contains all the essential tools for working with images, including the selection tools, brush tools, and type tools. At the top, you'll see the **Menu Bar**, which provides access to more advanced options like image adjustments, filters, and preferences. The **Options Bar** below the Menu Bar allows you to adjust settings for the currently selected tool. On the right, you'll find the **Panels**, such as Layers, History, and Properties, which give you more control over your image editing.

4. **Understanding Basic Tools and Functions**

   At this stage, you'll be introduced to some of Photoshop's most fundamental tools, such as the **Move Tool**, **Brush Tool**, **Crop Tool**, and **Lasso Tool**. These are the core tools you will use regularly in your projects. Take the time to experiment with them and become familiar with their functionality. We'll dive deeper into each of these tools throughout the book, explaining how to use them efficiently and effectively.

5. **Creating Your First Project**

   To get started, let's create a simple project: open an image in Photoshop 2025 and apply basic adjustments such as cropping, adjusting brightness and contrast, and adding text. By the time you complete this simple project, you will have gained a solid understanding of Photoshop's key features, allowing you to move on to more advanced techniques.

This book will take you step by step through the capabilities, tools, and methods of Adobe Photoshop 2025. Whether you're just starting out or you're trying to master new talents, you'll find everything you need here. Photoshop 2025 is a strong tool that may boost your creative work, and with the guidance of this guide, you'll be able to uncover its full potential.

The road from a Photoshop beginner to an expert might seem overwhelming, but with the correct tools and direction, you'll find that mastering Photoshop is not only doable but also gratifying. Now, let's begin your creative voyage and start mastering the fascinating world of Photoshop 2025!

Chapter 1

The Photoshop Interface – Your Creative Workspace

Did you realize that Adobe Photoshop has been around for more than 35 years? What started as a simple tool for image editing has developed into a multi-faceted powerhouse that millions of professionals and creatives use daily. In 2025, Photoshop continues to be the go-to tool for picture editing, graphic design, and digital art. With every update, Adobe refines its interface and functionality to make the creative process faster, more intuitive, and highly efficient.

For novices to Photoshop, the UI can seem intimidating. It's crammed with features, tools, and panels, each meant to enhance the user experience. However, with a little coaching, the Photoshop interface can become your most powerful partner. In this chapter, we will break down the Photoshop 2025 interface, explore its basic components, and teach you how to modify your workspace to make the application work for you.

Overview of Photoshop 2025 Interface

When you first use Photoshop 2025, you'll see a clean, modern workplace designed to provide maximum flexibility for a range of tasks. The interface is separated into numerous important parts, each providing a specific function in your creative process. Let's go over each of these topics in depth.

The Application Bar

The **Application Bar** is located at the top of the workspace. It contains essential functions that allow you to manage Photoshop as a whole. Here, you'll find:

- **Photoshop logo and file name**: On the left, you'll see the Photoshop logo, and to its right, the file name of the image you're working on.

- **Workspace switcher**: Photoshop allows you to switch between different workspaces depending on the task. For example, you can use the "Photography" workspace for photo editing or "Graphic and Web" for web design. You'll find a dropdown menu here to quickly switch between workspaces.

- **Search bar**: The integrated search bar (powered by Adobe Sensei) lets you search for tools, menu options, and even help articles without leaving the program. This feature is a huge time-saver when you're still learning the interface.

The Menu Bar

Beneath the **Application Bar**, you'll find the **Menu Bar**. It houses the traditional Photoshop menus that are the backbone of most commands:

- **File**: For opening, saving, and exporting documents.

- **Edit**: For undoing, cutting, pasting, and accessing other essential editing features.

- **Image**: For adjusting image size, resolution, and canvas settings.

- **Layer**: For layer-related actions, such as creating new layers, grouping layers, and managing layer effects.

- **Select**: For making selections in your document.

- **Filter**: To apply Photoshop's extensive library of filters and effects.

- **View**: To zoom, hide panels, and modify your workspace view.

- **Window**: To show or hide Photoshop's panels and other elements.

- **Help**: To access help documents and online tutorials.

Each of these menus contains more detailed options that we'll explore in later chapters. For now, it's essential to know that the **Menu Bar** is the starting point for most tasks within Photoshop.

The Toolbar

The Toolbar is undoubtedly the most famous component of Photoshop's interface. Located on the left side of the workspace, the Toolbar is packed with tools you'll use often for photo editing, painting, drawing, and much more. The Toolbar is customisable, allowing you to add or remove features depending on your workflow. Let's take a deeper look at the tools on the Toolbar.

Understanding the Toolbar: Tools You'll Use Daily

The Toolbar in Photoshop 2025 consists of two columns of icons. Each icon symbolizes a tool, and most tools include additional settings or variations that can be accessed by right-clicking or holding down the tool's icon. Some tools are grouped together under a single icon, which means that by clicking and holding on the icon, you can cycle among the numerous tools in that group.

Let's study the most important and commonly used features in the Photoshop Toolbar.

Move Tool (V)

The Move Tool is one of the most regularly used tools in Photoshop. It allows you to move layers, selections, and objects across your canvas. With the Move Tool, you can swiftly relocate text, images, and other objects, making it a crucial aspect of every Photoshop production.

Selection Tools

- **Marquee Tools (M)**: These tools allow you to make rectangular, elliptical, or single-pixel selections. They're great for isolating areas of your image to edit.

- **Lasso Tools (L)**: The **Lasso Tool** and its variations (Polygonal and Magnetic) allow you to make freeform selections around objects in your image. This is particularly useful when dealing with complex shapes or non-rectangular objects.

- **Quick Selection Tool (W)**: The **Quick Selection Tool** automatically detects edges and makes selections based on color and texture. It's fast and efficient for selecting large areas or areas with similar colors.

Brush Tool (B)

The **Brush Tool** is one of the most powerful tools in Photoshop. It's used for painting, erasing, and retouching. Whether you're painting a digital illustration or making minor corrections to a photo, the **Brush Tool** is indispensable. Photoshop allows you to customize the brush size, shape, and hardness, and you can even create your own custom brushes for unique effects.

Clone Stamp Tool (S)

The **Clone Stamp Tool** allows you to copy one area of an image and apply it to another. It's perfect for removing blemishes, duplicates, or unwanted objects in a photo. By holding **Alt** (or **Option** on Mac) and clicking on the source area, you can begin cloning.

Text Tool (T)

The **Text Tool** allows you to add, edit, and format text within your project. You can change the font, size, color, and alignment of your text to fit the style of your design. Photoshop also offers advanced text effects, such as drop shadows, gradients, and warping.

Eyedropper Tool (I)

The **Eyedropper Tool** lets you sample colors from your image and apply them to other elements. This tool is critical for ensuring color consistency and creating harmonious color schemes in your design.

Gradient Tool (G)

The **Gradient Tool** allows you to apply smooth color transitions to your image. Whether you're working on backgrounds, skies, or shading, the **Gradient Tool** adds depth and visual interest to your project.

Zoom Tool (Z)

The **Zoom Tool** allows you to zoom in and out of your document. It's essential when working on details in high-resolution images or when you need to examine specific areas of your design.

Hand Tool (H)

The **Hand Tool** is used for moving around your canvas when you're zoomed in on an area. It's a simple but essential tool for navigating large images without losing your place.

These are just a few of the core tools available in the **Toolbar**. As you work through the guide, you'll become more familiar with each tool's capabilities and how they can enhance your projects.

Customizing Your Workspace: Making Photoshop Work for You

One of the most significant features of Photoshop is its ability to personalize the workspace to match your needs. As you become more acquainted with Photoshop, you'll likely establish a preferred process, and the good news is that Photoshop allows you to adjust the interface to make your work faster and more efficient.

Workspace Presets

Photoshop comes with many workspace presets that are suited for specific purposes. For example, the Photography workspace is tailored for photo editing, featuring panels and tools that are most typically used in photography. Similarly, the Graphics and Web workspace is optimized for graphic design jobs.

To switch between these workspaces, simply go to **Window > Workspace,** and choose your chosen layout. If you discover that none of the presets satisfy your needs, you can also construct your own personalized workspace.

Arranging Panels

Photoshop's Panels are a vital element of your workflow. They allow access to tools like Layers, **Adjustments, History, and Properties.** You can move, resize, and conceal these panels to make more area for your work. If you're working on a huge project with numerous panels open, consider using the Tab key to hide all the panels at once and focus just on the image.

To modify your panels, simply go to Window and check the panels you require. You may slide them around to different regions of your screen or dock them to one side for convenient access. Photoshop also remembers your arrangement, so when you open the software again, your panels will be positioned just as you left them.

Creating Custom Shortcuts

Photoshop allows you to assign custom keyboard shortcuts to frequently used tools or commands. This can significantly speed up your workflow, especially if you're working on repetitive tasks. To assign a custom shortcut, go to **Edit > Keyboard Shortcuts**, and choose the action you want to assign a shortcut to.

Saving Custom Workspaces

Once you've customized your workspace and tools, you can save the layout for future use. Go to **Window > Workspace > New Workspace**, and Photoshop will store your layout so you can quickly switch back to it at any time. This is perfect for designers who need different setups for different tasks, such as photo retouching, web design, or digital painting.

The Menu Bar, Options Bar, and Panels

These three elements make up the foundation of your workspace in Photoshop. They provide you with access to all the features and functions that Photoshop has to offer. Let's explore each one in detail.

The Menu Bar

The **Menu Bar** is the main hub for accessing Photoshop's functions. Located at the top of your workspace, it contains various dropdown menus that control everything from file management to complex image editing. The Menu Bar is broken down into several categories:

- **File**: This menu provides access to basic file operations like creating, opening, saving, and printing documents. It also contains export options, including saving your work as different file types (e.g., PSD, JPEG, PNG).

- **Edit**: The Edit menu includes commands for editing your image or document. This is where you'll find essential actions like cutting, copying, pasting, and undoing changes. You can also access preferences and other customization settings here.

- **Image**: This menu is dedicated to adjustments and modifications at the image level. You can adjust your image's size, resolution, and canvas settings from here. It's also where you'll find color correction options, such as brightness/contrast, levels, and curves.

- **Layer**: Layers are a core component of Photoshop, and this menu controls all layer-related functions. Here, you can add, delete, group, and merge layers, as well as adjust their blending modes and opacity.

- **Select**: The Select menu provides options for selecting specific areas of your image. You can use the Marquee tools, lasso tools, or other selection methods to isolate areas for editing. You'll also find options for modifying or refining selections in this menu.

- **Filter**: This is where you'll find Photoshop's wide range of filters. Filters are used to apply visual effects, such as blurring, sharpening, and distortion. You'll also find artistic filters and other specialized effects here.

- **View**: The View menu controls how your image is displayed on the screen. You can zoom in or out, change the resolution, and even adjust how the panels and tools appear.

- **Window**: The Window menu lets you manage the panels and interface elements. You can open, close, or rearrange panels according to your preferences, which is essential for customizing your workspace.

- **Help**: For troubleshooting, tutorials, and other resources, the Help menu provides easy access to Photoshop's built-in help system.

The **Menu Bar** is your gateway to nearly all of Photoshop's functions, and being familiar with these menus will significantly enhance your workflow.

The Options Bar

Located directly below the Menu Bar, the **Options Bar** dynamically updates depending on the tool you have selected. It's an essential part of your workflow because it gives you quick access to tool-specific settings and adjustments. For example:

- If you select the **Brush Tool**, the Options Bar will display settings for **brush size**, **hardness**, **spacing**, and **mode**.

- When using the **Text Tool**, the Options Bar will show **font, size, color**, and **alignment** options.

- If you choose the **Zoom Tool**, the Options Bar allows you to adjust the zoom level with a slider or toggle between zooming in and out.

The **Options Bar** saves you time by eliminating the need to dig through menus to find tool-specific settings. You can fine-tune the selected tool's properties directly from this bar, which is especially helpful when you're working with a variety of tools.

The Panels

On the right side of your screen, you'll find the **Panels**. These panels are essential for controlling various aspects of your image and workflow. There are several panels in Photoshop, but the most commonly used ones include:

- **Layers Panel**: This is perhaps the most important panel in Photoshop. It shows all of the layers in your document, allowing you to manipulate each one individually. You can adjust the opacity, blending mode, and visibility of layers, as well as group and organize them.

- **Adjustments Panel**: This panel provides easy access to non-destructive adjustments, such as brightness/contrast, hue/saturation, and curves. You can apply these adjustments to specific layers without permanently altering the original image.

- **Properties Panel**: The **Properties Panel** offers additional options for selected layers or tools. For example, if you have a shape layer selected, the **Properties Panel** will let you adjust the fill and stroke color. For text layers, you can change the font, size, and alignment.

- **History Panel**: The **History Panel** tracks every action you take in Photoshop. This allows you to go back to previous steps in your editing process. It's especially useful for undoing changes or experimenting with different techniques without permanently altering your image.

- **Tools Panel**: On the left side of your workspace, you'll find the **Tools Panel**, which contains a wide range of editing tools. From here, you can select tools like the Brush Tool, Clone Stamp, Lasso Tool, and more. Many tools are grouped together in the **Tools Panel**, and you can access hidden tools by clicking and holding the tool icon.

You can change which panels appear on your workspace by heading to the Window menu. You may also arrange and dock panels to keep your workplace tidy, ensuring you have easy access to the tools and settings you use most often.

2. Navigating Your Canvas: Zooming, Panning, and Grid Setup

Now that we've covered the fundamental features of the Menu Bar, Options Bar, and Panels, let's delve into how you interact with your image on the canvas. Navigating your canvas effectively is vital for precise editing, and Photoshop includes various tools and shortcuts for this.

Zooming

Zooming in and out helps you to have a closer look at your image's details or to examine the overall composition. There are a few different approaches to zoom in Photoshop:

- **Using the Zoom Tool**: Select the **Zoom Tool** from the **Tools Panel** or press the **Z** key on your keyboard. Click on the area of the image you want to zoom in on. To zoom out, hold the **Alt** key (Windows) or **Option** key (Mac) while clicking. You can also click and drag to zoom in on a specific area.

- **Keyboard Shortcuts**: Press **Ctrl + (Plus)** (Windows) or **Cmd + (Plus)** (Mac) to zoom in. To zoom out, press **Ctrl + (Minus)** (Windows) or **Cmd + (Minus)** (Mac).

- **Mouse Scroll Wheel**: If you have a mouse with a scroll wheel, hold the **Alt** key (Windows) or **Option** key (Mac) and scroll the wheel up to zoom in or down to zoom out.

Using zoom efficiently is critical when you're working with detailed artwork or trying to fine-tune your edits.

Panning

When working with high-resolution images, you'll often need to move around your canvas to see different parts of the image. Here are a few ways to pan within Photoshop:

- **Using the Hand Tool**: Select the **Hand Tool** from the **Tools Panel** or press the **H** key on your keyboard. Click and drag your image to move it around the canvas.

- **Spacebar Shortcut**: Hold down the **Spacebar** while using any tool, and Photoshop will temporarily switch to the **Hand Tool**. This allows you to quickly pan around your image while keeping the other tool active.

- **Mouse Scroll Wheel**: In combination with the **Ctrl** (Windows) or **Cmd** (Mac) key, you can hold the **Spacebar** and scroll the mouse wheel to pan across the canvas.

Panning is an important aspect of working on large projects, as it allows you to explore different parts of your document without losing your place.

Grid Setup

Setting up grids helps you align elements with precision, whether you're designing a web layout, positioning text, or creating a composition. Here's how to set up grids in Photoshop:

- **Turning On the Grid**: Go to **View > Show > Grid** to display a grid on your canvas. This grid will help you align your elements based on a series of horizontal and vertical lines.

- **Customizing the Grid**: To change the grid's settings, go to **Edit > Preferences > Guides, Grid & Slices** (Windows) or **Photoshop > Preferences > Guides, Grid & Slices** (Mac). You can adjust the grid's **spacing**, **color**, and **style** to suit your needs.

- **Snapping to the Grid**: To ensure that your elements snap to the grid lines, go to **View > Snap To** and choose **Grid**. This will make it easier to align your images or shapes with the grid.

3. Shortcuts and Efficiency Hacks for Beginners

Using shortcuts is one of the best ways to increase your productivity in Photoshop. Here are some essential shortcuts that every beginner should learn:

- **Ctrl + Z** (Windows) or **Cmd + Z** (Mac): **Undo** the last action. Pressing this multiple times will step backward through your previous actions.

- **Ctrl + Alt + Z** (Windows) or **Cmd + Option + Z** (Mac): **Step backward** through multiple actions.

- **Ctrl + Shift + Z** (Windows) or **Cmd + Shift + Z** (Mac): **Redo** the action you just undid.

- **Ctrl + T** (Windows) or **Cmd + T** (Mac): **Free Transform**. This allows you to resize, rotate, and skew your selected layers.

- **Ctrl + J** (Windows) or **Cmd + J** (Mac): **Duplicate layer**.

- **Ctrl + D** (Windows) or **Cmd + D** (Mac): **Deselect** your selection.

- **Alt + Scroll Wheel** (Windows) or **Option + Scroll Wheel** (Mac): **Zoom in/out**.

By learning and incorporating these shortcuts into your workflow, you'll find yourself editing much faster and more efficiently.

Understanding the Photoshop interface and learning how to configure your workspace, browse your canvas, and utilize vital shortcuts are key steps in becoming adept with the software. In this chapter, we've examined the core aspects of the Menu Bar, Options Bar, and Panels, as well as how to zoom, pan, and set up grids to work more accurately. With these tools and strategies, you'll be able to approach Photoshop with confidence and start working more efficiently.

Chapter 2

Mastering Photoshop Basics – Essential Tools and Techniques

Photoshop is a diverse and powerful tool, but to really exploit its powers, understanding the fundamentals is crucial. In this chapter, we'll dive into the underlying parts that make up Photoshop's core capabilities. Whether you're retouching a portrait, constructing a website, or producing a digital artwork, these foundations will establish the groundwork for more sophisticated approaches.

One of the most powerful parts of Photoshop is its non-destructive editing capabilities, partly made possible by the usage of layers. Layers enable flexibility in editing and allow you to make alterations without permanently affecting the source image. This principle of working non-destructively is one of the key reasons Photoshop has become the industry standard for photo editing and design.

Additionally, picking certain sections of an image for editing is another vital ability. In this chapter, we'll study the numerous selection tools in Photoshop and how they give you the capacity to isolate and alter areas of an image with accuracy.

Lastly, the Brush Tool in Photoshop is vital for activities ranging from painting and retouching to designing intricate designs. Understanding how to use brushes, customize them, and work with painting tools will help you to produce art with ease.

By the end of this chapter, you'll be equipped with the knowledge to deal with layers, make correct choices, and apply brushes efficiently, forming the foundation for your Photoshop talents.

Layers and Their Importance in Photoshop

In Photoshop, layers are one of the most crucial functions. A layer is essentially a single image or object that may be edited independently of the others. Working with layers is like stacking translucent sheets of paper, where each sheet contains a component of the image. Layers can be changed, moved, hidden, or destroyed without impacting the rest of the image, offering a non-destructive process that makes Photoshop an exceptionally effective tool for creative professionals.

What Are Layers?

Each image in Photoshop is built of one or more layers. When you open a photo, it's placed on the Background Layer by default. However, whenever you start adding more items, such as text, shapes, or tweaks, each element is placed on a distinct layer.

There are several types of layers in Photoshop:

- **Background Layer**: The background layer is typically the bottom-most layer of your image. It is usually locked, meaning you can't move it or delete it unless you convert it to a regular layer.

- **Image Layers**: These are the layers that contain your photos, graphics, and other visual elements. You can move, scale, and adjust them independently.

- **Text Layers**: If you add text to your image, Photoshop creates a **text layer**, which you can edit and format without affecting the rest of the image.

- **Adjustment Layers**: Adjustment layers allow you to apply effects such as brightness/contrast, hue/saturation, and curves without altering the original image layer. They are incredibly useful for making non-destructive edits.

- **Shape Layers**: Any vector-based shapes you create are placed on their own layer, making it easy to adjust their size, color, or position without affecting the rest of the image.

Why Layers Are Important

Working with layers gives you **full creative control** over your image. Here are some reasons why layers are indispensable in Photoshop:

- **Non-destructive editing**: Layers allow you to make changes to specific elements of an image without permanently altering the underlying photo. For example, you can adjust the color or brightness of an image using an **Adjustment Layer**, and if you don't like the result, you can simply delete the adjustment layer without affecting the original image.

- **Flexibility**: Layers provide the ability to move, scale, and rotate individual elements of an image. You can even apply different blending modes to create various visual effects, such as adding shadows or highlights to specific parts of the image.

- **Organizing your workflow**: Layers make it easier to manage complex projects. By grouping related layers together, you can organize your work and make it easier to locate specific elements.

- **Reversibility**: Unlike traditional image editing methods, where changes are permanent, layers allow you to go back to any point in the editing process. You can hide, lock, or delete layers to quickly undo changes.

Layer Techniques

To maximize your use of layers, here are a few key techniques:

- **Layer Masks**: A **Layer Mask** allows you to hide parts of a layer without permanently deleting them. By painting with black, you can hide parts of the layer; painting with white will bring them back. This is especially useful for creating seamless blends or correcting mistakes.

- **Blending Modes**: Blending modes determine how a layer blends with the layers beneath it. For example, the **Multiply** blending mode darkens an image, while **Screen** lightens it. Blending modes are essential for creating special effects, such as glowing lights or shadowing.

- **Layer Styles**: Photoshop offers various built-in layer styles, such as **drop shadows**, **outer glows**, and **embossing**. You can apply these effects to layers, creating dimension and depth in your work.

Working with Selections: Marquee, Lasso, and Quick Selection Tools

Selections are a crucial component of the editing process in Photoshop. A selection allows you to isolate a specific portion of an image, making it feasible to make edits or effects to just that part of the image without impacting the rest. Photoshop includes various selection tools, each with its own strengths and use cases. Let's explore the Marquee, Lasso, and Quick Selection tools.

The Marquee Tools

The **Marquee Tools** are used to make rectangular or elliptical selections. There are two primary types of Marquee tools:

- **Rectangular Marquee Tool (M)**: This tool allows you to make rectangular selections. Simply click and drag to select an area.

- **Elliptical Marquee Tool (M)**: Similar to the rectangular marquee, but it allows you to select elliptical areas. To create a perfect circle, hold down the **Shift** key while dragging.

The **Marquee Tools** are great for selecting areas with regular, straight-edged shapes. However, they can be limiting when it comes to more complex shapes.

The Lasso Tools

The **Lasso Tools** provide more flexibility when making freeform selections. There are three variations of the Lasso Tool:

- **Lasso Tool (L)**: The basic Lasso Tool allows you to draw a selection around any shape or object. Simply click and drag to outline the area you want to select.

- **Polygonal Lasso Tool (L)**: This tool allows you to make straight-edged selections. Click to create a corner point, and Photoshop will automatically connect the dots to create a straight line. It's ideal for selecting objects with angular edges.

- **Magnetic Lasso Tool (L)**: The Magnetic Lasso Tool automatically detects the edges of objects and "snaps" the selection to them. This is especially useful when working with images that have high contrast between the subject and the background, like a person with dark hair against a light background.

The **Lasso Tools** are excellent for selecting irregular shapes or areas that don't fit the standard rectangular or elliptical patterns.

The Quick Selection Tool

The **Quick Selection Tool (W)** is one of the most powerful and easiest-to-use selection tools in Photoshop. This tool automatically detects edges in your image and allows you to paint over the area you want to select. As you drag the tool, it will expand the selection to include similar colors and textures, making it an excellent choice for selecting complex subjects like a person's face or an animal.

- **Refining Selections**: Once you've made your selection, you can refine it by using the **Select and Mask** workspace, which allows you to adjust the edges of your selection, smoothing, feathering, or contracting it for a more polished result.

- **Adding to or Subtracting from Selections**: Hold down the **Shift** key to add to a selection or the **Alt** (Windows) / **Option** (Mac) key to subtract from it.

Selection Tips and Tricks

- **Feathering**: Feathering softens the edges of a selection, giving it a smoother transition between the selected area and the rest of the image. You can adjust the feather amount in the options bar or the **Select > Modify > Feather** menu.

- **Saving Selections**: If you've made a complex selection and want to save it for later use, go to **Select > Save Selection**. This will save your selection as a channel, which you can load again at any time.

- **Refining Edges**: For selections with hard-to-define edges, such as hair or fur, use the **Select and Mask** workspace. This workspace provides tools to refine edges and create more accurate selections.

Basic Brush Techniques: Painting, Editing, and Customizing Brushes

The Brush Tool (B) is a fundamental feature of Photoshop, utilized for activities such as painting, retouching, and crafting complex details. The Brush Tool's efficacy stems from its adaptability; it is adept at painting landscapes, retouching portraits, and making logos alike. Let us examine the effective utilization of it.

Utilizing the Brush Tool for Painting

To commence painting with the Brush Tool, choose it from the Tools Panel and begin applying it to your canvas. The brush size, hardness, and opacity can be adjusted in the Options Bar to create various effects:

- **Brush Size**: Use the size slider in the **Options Bar** or use the keyboard shortcut [(smaller) and] (larger) to adjust the size of your brush.

- **Hardness**: Hardness controls the edge of your brush. A **hard brush** will have sharp, defined edges, while a **soft brush** creates smooth, blurred edges.

- **Opacity**: Opacity controls the transparency of your brush strokes. Lower opacity creates softer, more subtle strokes, while higher opacity provides solid, fully opaque strokes.

You can also adjust the **flow** and **spacing** of the brush for more control over how your strokes are applied.

Editing with the Brush Tool

In addition to painting, the **Brush Tool** can be used for editing. It's ideal for tasks such as:

- **Retouching skin** in a portrait.

- **Blurring edges** or creating a soft focus effect.

- **Dodging and burning**, which means lightening or darkening specific areas of an image to add depth or highlight details.

To switch between different **brush presets** in Photoshop, open the **Brush Preset Picker** from the **Options Bar**. Photoshop comes with a variety of brushes for different effects, from soft airbrushes to textured brushes that simulate natural painting techniques.

Customizing Brushes

One of the most powerful features of the Brush Tool is the ability to **customize brushes** to fit your needs:

- **Brush Settings Panel**: Go to **Window > Brush Settings** to open the **Brush Settings Panel**, where you can modify settings like shape, angle, roundness, and spacing. You can also adjust dynamic settings like **scattering**, **texture**, and **dual brush** combinations.

- **Creating Custom Brushes**: You can create your own custom brushes by selecting a shape or image and defining it as a brush. This allows you to create unique effects that suit your specific project.

- **Brush Tip Shape**: You can modify the shape of the brush tip itself to create different stroke effects, whether you need a soft, round brush or a textured, irregular pattern.

Color Theory: Understanding the Color Wheel, Color Picker, and Swatches

One of the fundamental abilities in digital design and photo editing is understanding color theory. Colors affect our perception of images and can express emotions, establish moods, and provide harmony or contrast. Proficiency in color selection tools such as the Color Wheel, Color Picker, and Swatches in Photoshop is crucial for creating aesthetically pleasing and impactful designs.

What constitutes Color Theory?

Color theory is the study of how colors interact with one other. It entails understanding how to blend colors in a way that provides aesthetically pleasant outcomes. The basis of color theory resides in the color wheel, which is a circular pattern of colors grouped by their chromatic relationship. By using the color wheel, designers can develop harmonious color schemes that convey the correct tone for their work.

There are several key concepts in color theory that you'll encounter in Photoshop:

- **Primary Colors**: Red, blue, and yellow. These colors cannot be created by mixing other colors and are the foundation for creating all other colors.

- **Secondary Colors**: Green, orange, and purple. These colors are created by mixing two primary colors.

- **Tertiary Colors**: These are created by mixing a primary color with a secondary color, such as red-orange or blue-green.

- **Complementary Colors**: These are pairs of colors that are opposite each other on the color wheel, like blue and orange or red and green. Complementary colors create high contrast and are often used to make certain elements of a design stand out.

- **Analogous Colors**: These colors sit next to each other on the color wheel, such as blue, blue-green, and green. They tend to create a harmonious and serene effect when used together.

- **Monochromatic Colors**: Variations of a single color, including its tints, shades, and tones. Using monochromatic colors creates a clean and cohesive look.

The Color Picker Tool

In Photoshop, the **Color Picker** is one of the most important tools for selecting colors. It allows you to choose the perfect color for your image or design. You can access the **Color Picker** by clicking on the foreground or background color boxes at the bottom of the **Tools Panel**.

The **Color Picker** has several key components:

- **Hue**: The color itself (such as red, green, or blue) is represented by a bar at the top of the Color Picker. You can slide the pointer to select a hue.

- **Saturation**: The intensity of the color. Moving the pointer along the vertical slider will adjust how vivid the color appears.

- **Brightness**: Controls how light or dark the color is.

- **Hexadecimal Code**: At the bottom of the Color Picker, you'll see a 6-digit code that represents the color. This is useful when you need to match exact colors for branding or web design.

Photoshop also provides an option to switch between RGB and HSL color models, which is useful for different types of design work.

Using Swatches for Color Management

Once you've selected a color in the **Color Picker**, you can save it to the **Swatches Panel** for future use. This is especially helpful when you're working with a consistent color palette throughout a project, such as creating a logo or web design. To add a color to your swatches:

1. Select the color in the **Color Picker**.

2. Open the **Swatches Panel (Window > Swatches)**.

3. Click the **New Swatch** button at the bottom of the panel to save the color.

You can create custom swatches for your project by adding frequently used colors and even importing swatches from other projects or external sources.

By mastering the **Color Picker**, **Swatches**, and understanding **color theory**, you'll be able to choose and manage colors with precision, creating harmonious and engaging designs.

Masks and Adjustments: Why and When to Use Them

In Photoshop, masks and adjustments are crucial tools that provide you creative freedom and non-destructive editing capabilities. They let you make modifications to particular portions of your image without affecting the original pixels. Learning how and when to apply masks and adjustments will substantially enhance your efficiency and the quality of your work.

What are Masks?

A mask in Photoshop is a technique of hiding or showing elements of a layer without permanently destroying any information. Masks are commonly referred to as non-destructive editing tools since they provide you the opportunity to edit areas of your image or layer without making permanent changes. By utilizing a mask, you can paint over parts of a layer to hide or show areas as desired.

There are two main types of masks:

- **Layer Mask**: This is the most common type of mask. It is linked to a specific layer and controls which areas of that layer are visible. A black mask hides the layer, a white mask shows the entire layer, and gray shades create partial transparency.

- **Clipping Mask**: A clipping mask allows you to apply an effect or adjustment to a specific layer based on the layer below it. This technique is helpful when you want to limit adjustments to a particular area of the image or layer.

How to use a Layer Mask:

1. Select the layer you want to apply the mask to.

2. Click the **Add Layer Mask** button at the bottom of the Layers Panel.

3. Paint on the mask using the **Brush Tool**. Use black to hide areas, white to reveal areas, and gray for partial transparency.

Masks are incredibly powerful for creating complex composites, retouching images, or applying subtle effects without permanent changes.

Adjustment Layers: Non-Destructive Editing

Adjustment layers in Photoshop allow you to apply color and tone modifications to your image in a non-destructive fashion. These layers do not modify the source image but instead add an overlay of adjustment that can be adjusted or removed at any moment. Adjustment layers are vital for fine-tuning photographs, whether you're tweaking the brightness, contrast, or color balance.

Common adjustment layers include:

- **Brightness/Contrast**: Adjusts the overall brightness and contrast of the image.

- **Hue/Saturation**: Alters the hue, saturation, and lightness of the image, perfect for color correction or creative color shifts.

- **Levels and Curves**: Used to adjust the shadows, midtones, and highlights of an image. Curves offer more precise control over tonal adjustments.

- **Black & White**: Converts the image to grayscale while giving you control over how each color channel is converted.

To apply an adjustment layer:

1. Go to **Layer > New Adjustment Layer** and choose the adjustment you want to apply.

2. The adjustment layer will appear above your image layer in the Layers Panel. You can modify its properties by clicking on the adjustment thumbnail in the Layers Panel.

Adjustment layers are crucial when you want to make global changes to your image but still retain full control over the original content.

Why and When to Use Masks and Adjustments

Masks and adjustments are essential for non-destructive editing. Here's why they are valuable:

- **Flexibility**: Masks give you the ability to experiment with different effects without committing to them. If you don't like an effect, simply adjust the mask or delete it.

- **Precision**: Masks allow you to target specific areas of an image for edits, which means you can apply selective changes with great precision.

- **Reversibility**: Adjustment layers can be edited, disabled, or deleted at any time without impacting the original image. This gives you the freedom to experiment with your edits without fear of permanent mistakes.

Saving and Exporting Files: PSD vs. JPEG, PNG, and More

Saving and exporting your work in Photoshop is just as vital as modifying it. Different file formats are used for different purposes, and knowing which format to use will save you time and ensure your photographs preserve their quality.

PSD vs. JPEG, PNG, and Other File Formats

The most prevalent file formats used in Photoshop are PSD, JPEG, PNG, and TIFF. Each format has its particular advantages and purposes. Let's investigate each one in more detail.

PSD (Photoshop Document)

A PSD file is the native file format of Photoshop. When you save your work in this format, it keeps all layers, masks, modifications, and other editing tools, allowing you to go back and edit your project at any time. This format is essential for working on complex files that you need to update or revise later.

Advantages:

- **Preserves layers and edits**: Retains all the layers, masks, and adjustment layers, allowing you to continue editing the file later.

- **Non-destructive editing**: Because it keeps all your layers intact, you can make changes without losing quality or information.

Disadvantages:

- **Large file size**: PSD files tend to be larger than other file formats because they retain all the layers and editing information.

JPEG (Joint Photographic Experts Group)

JPEG is one of the most extensively used file formats for preserving photographs, especially for web use and sharing on social media. It employs lossy compression, meaning that some image data is deleted to minimize file size. JPEGs are appropriate for photographs and images where file size is more critical than maintaining every detail.

Advantages:

- **Small file size**: Ideal for web use, email, and sharing images online.

- **Widely compatible**: JPEGs can be opened and viewed on almost any device.

Disadvantages:

- **Loss of quality**: JPEGs lose some image quality due to compression, which can result in artifacts or visible pixelation, especially at lower quality settings.

PNG (Portable Network Graphics)

PNG is a lossless image format that supports transparent backgrounds, making it perfect for logos, graphics, and images that require transparency. It retains full image quality without any loss due to compression.

Advantages:

- **Lossless compression**: Retains image quality with no data loss.

- **Transparency support**: Ideal for images with transparent backgrounds.

Disadvantages:

- **Larger file size**: PNG files are typically larger than JPEG files, especially for images with lots of detail.

Other Formats

- **TIFF**: A high-quality file format commonly used in print production. It retains high detail and image quality but is often large in size.

- **GIF**: Best for animated images or images with fewer colors.

In this chapter, we've covered three key parts of Photoshop that every user needs to master: color theory, masks and changes, and saving and exporting files. By understanding how to work with color, make accurate selections, and apply adjustment layers, you'll obtain the creative power needed to produce professional-quality designs and photographs.

Additionally, knowing when and how to save your work in the correct format ensures that your products preserve their quality and are available for sharing, printing, or additional editing.

Chapter 3

Image Editing Techniques – Beyond the Basics

In the world of digital art and photo editing, going beyond basic adjustments and entering the realm of fine-tuned, professional-level alterations may make all the difference in the quality of your work. With Adobe Photoshop 2025, you have a huge selection of tools and techniques at your disposal to change your photographs from good to great. Whether you're a photographer, designer, or digital artist, understanding these advanced image editing techniques will help you enhance your talents and generate spectacular outcomes.

In this chapter, we will study the sophisticated tools and approaches that go beyond basic editing. We'll start with retouching techniques, including the Healing Brush, Clone Stamp, and Patch Tool, which allow you to erase defects and make exact alterations. We'll then dig into working with text—adding, formatting, and decorating text layers to enhance your designs. Lastly, we'll look at Smart Objects, a vital idea for non-destructive editing, which allows you to make changes without permanently affecting your original image.

By the end of this chapter, you'll be equipped with advanced techniques that can take your photographs to a professional level and improve your whole workflow.

Retouching Photos: Healing Brush, Clone Stamp, and Patch Tool

Photo retouching is one of the most common activities in Photoshop, whether you're increasing the quality of a photograph, removing distractions from an image, or making minor edits. The Healing Brush, Clone Stamp, and Patch Tool are powerful tools in Photoshop that allow you to erase blemishes, mend defects, and flawlessly merge portions of an image. Let's take a look at each of these tools in depth.

Healing Brush Tool (J)

The Healing Brush Tool is one of Photoshop's most powerful retouching tools. It's typically used for erasing blemishes, scars, and other flaws from photos. What sets the Healing Brush Tool unique from other cloning tools is its ability to integrate the sampled texture, color, and lighting with the surrounding region. This makes it an ideal alternative for skin retouching or repairing defects in images.

How to Use the Healing Brush Tool:

1. **Select the Healing Brush Tool** from the **Tools Panel** or press **J** on your keyboard.

2. In the **Options Bar**, choose the appropriate **brush size**. A soft, round brush works best for smooth blending.

3. Hold **Alt** (Windows) or **Option** (Mac) and click on a clean area of the image to sample the texture.

4. Paint over the area you want to retouch. Photoshop will blend the sampled texture with the surrounding pixels.

The **Healing Brush Tool** works well on small areas, such as removing blemishes from skin or cleaning up dust spots. It's especially useful when you need a quick, seamless fix.

Clone Stamp Tool (S)

The **Clone Stamp Tool** is another crucial tool for photo retouching. Unlike the Healing Brush Tool, the Clone Stamp Tool repeats the precise pixels from one part of an image and places them elsewhere. This makes it perfect for removing major distractions, replicating things, or repairing sections with a uniform texture.

How to Use the Clone Stamp Tool:

1. **Select the Clone Stamp Tool** from the **Tools Panel** or press **S** on your keyboard.

2. In the **Options Bar**, adjust the **brush size**, **hardness**, and **opacity** to fit your needs.

3. Hold **Alt** (Windows) or **Option** (Mac) and click to sample an area of the image.

4. Paint over the area you want to fix. The sampled pixels will be duplicated exactly onto the new area.

The **Clone Stamp Tool** is especially useful for more complex fixes, such as removing large objects from the background or replacing missing parts of an image. It provides precision, but it requires careful attention to ensure the cloned area matches the surrounding textures and colors.

Patch Tool (J)

The **Patch Tool** is a versatile retouching tool that combines the functionality of both the **Healing Brush Tool** and **Clone Stamp Tool**. It's used to repair larger areas of an image by sampling pixels from another part of the image or using surrounding textures for seamless blending. The

Patch Tool is great for fixing areas with more complex textures or patterns, such as replacing a damaged area in a textured surface.

How to Use the Patch Tool:

1. **Select the Patch Tool** from the **Tools Panel** or press **J** (it may be grouped with the Healing Brush Tool).

2. In the **Options Bar**, choose either **Source** or **Destination**:

   ○ **Source**: You'll select the area you want to fix and drag it to a clean area of the image.

   ○ **Destination**: You'll drag a clean area over the area you want to repair.

3. After selecting the area you want to repair, drag the selection to a clean, similar area.

4. Photoshop will blend the selected pixels with the surrounding area, making the repair seamless.

The **Patch Tool** is ideal for larger, more complex fixes and allows you to repair textures and gradients without leaving visible seams.

Working with Text: Adding, Formatting, and Styling Text Layers

Text is an essential component in many design projects, from generating website banners to producing social media visuals. Photoshop includes a number of tools for inserting, formatting, and styling text to produce professional designs that stand out. In this section, we'll look at how to add text to your photos, format it for clarity and style, and apply effects to enhance its appearance.

Adding Text to Your Image

To add text to an image, Photoshop provides the **Text Tool** (T). The **Text Tool** allows you to create both point text (single line) and paragraph text (multiple lines).

How to Add Text:

1. Select the **Text Tool** from the **Tools Panel** or press **T** on your keyboard.

2. Click anywhere on your canvas where you want to add text.

3. Type the text you want to add to the image.

4. Photoshop automatically creates a **text layer** in the Layers Panel. This layer is editable, meaning you can change the text, font, size, and color at any time.

Once the text is added, you can use the **Move Tool** (V) to reposition it, and the **Transform** options (Ctrl + T / Cmd + T) to resize, rotate, or skew it.

Formatting and Styling Text

After adding text, Photoshop offers a wealth of options to format and style it. You can adjust the **font**, **size**, **weight**, and **tracking**, as well as apply **kerning** and **leading** adjustments to ensure proper spacing between characters and lines of text.

How to Format Text:

1. Select the **Text Tool** and highlight the text you want to format.

2. Use the **Options Bar** to adjust font, size, and alignment.

3. For more advanced formatting, open the **Character** panel (**Window > Character**) to adjust kerning, tracking, and other text attributes.

4. You can also change the **color** of your text by clicking the color box in the **Options Bar**.

Applying Text Effects

Once your text is formatted, you can apply various styles and effects to make it stand out. **Layer Styles** are a quick and easy way to apply effects such as drop shadows, glows, and bevels.

How to Apply Layer Styles:

1. Right-click on the text layer in the Layers Panel.

2. Select **Blending Options**.

3. From the **Layer Style** menu, you can add a **Drop Shadow, Outer Glow, Bevel and Emboss**, and more.

4. Adjust the settings for each effect to achieve the desired look.

Text effects are an excellent way to add emphasis or create a unique visual style for your text-based designs.

Using Smart Objects for Non-Destructive Editing

One of Photoshop's most powerful features is Smart Objects, which allows you to perform non-destructive editing. When you convert a layer to a Smart Object, any transformation, filter, or effect applied to it can be adjusted or removed at any moment. This retains the original data, enabling you to make modifications without permanently affecting the underlying material.

What Are Smart Objects?

A Smart Object is a layer that contains picture data from raster or vector images. Smart Objects allow you to apply transformations, filters, and modifications without permanently affecting the underlying data. This non-destructive technique is very handy when dealing with several layers or when you need to protect the quality of your source photos.

How to Create a Smart Object:

1. Right-click on the layer in the Layers Panel.

2. Select **Convert to Smart Object**. This will convert the selected layer into a Smart Object.

3. You'll notice a small icon on the layer thumbnail, indicating that it is a Smart Object.

Benefits of Smart Objects

- **Non-Destructive Editing**: Any adjustments or filters you apply to a Smart Object can be edited or removed without affecting the original image.

- **Re-scaling Without Quality Loss**: When you resize a Smart Object, Photoshop preserves its original quality. This means you can resize an image as much as you like without worrying about pixelation or distortion.

- **Smart Filters**: Smart Objects allow you to apply **Smart Filters**, which are editable filters that can be modified or turned off at any time. For example, you can apply a **Gaussian Blur** or **Sharpen** filter to a Smart Object, and if you don't like the result, you can double-click on the filter and adjust its settings.

Working with Smart Filters:

1. Once you've converted a layer to a Smart Object, you can apply filters just like you would to any other layer.

2. To apply a Smart Filter, go to **Filter > Filter Gallery** or use any of the built-in Photoshop filters.

3. The filter will appear below the Smart Object in the Layers Panel.

4. You can double-click the filter in the Layers Panel to adjust its settings or click the **eye icon** next to it to toggle it on or off.

Smart Objects and Smart Filters make it easier to experiment with different effects and transformations without compromising the quality of your original image.

Advanced Selection Methods: Refine Edge and Quick Mask

Making precise selections is one of the most fundamental and vital abilities in Photoshop. Whether you're dealing with portraits, landscapes, or composites, the ability to isolate and modify certain sections of a picture is crucial. Photoshop has a range of selection tools to assist you accomplish this, but sophisticated techniques like Refine Edge and Quick Mask add an extra degree of precision, especially when dealing with complex selections.

Refine Edge: Perfecting Selections

The Refine Edge tool (now included into Select and Mask) is one of the most effective capabilities in Photoshop for improving the edges of your choices. This tool is especially helpful when you're selecting fine elements like hair, fur, or soft edges that are difficult to isolate with regular selection tools. It works by recognizing the transition between the targeted area and its surroundings, allowing you to make smooth, natural selections.

How to Use Refine Edge:

1. **Make a Selection**: Start by using any selection tool (e.g., **Quick Selection Tool**, **Magic Wand**, or **Lasso Tool**) to select the area you want to isolate.

2. **Open Select and Mask**: With the selection active, go to **Select > Select and Mask** to open the Select and Mask workspace.

3. **Refine the Edges**: In the **Select and Mask** workspace, you'll see a variety of options for refining your selection:

   o **Radius**: Adjusts the softness of the selection edge. Increasing the radius can help capture more detail, such as fine hair or soft transitions.

   o **Edge Detection**: This feature allows Photoshop to identify and refine the edges of the selection, especially in areas with high contrast.

   o **Smooth, Feather, and Contrast**: These sliders refine the edge of the selection by adjusting smoothness, feathering (softness), and contrast for a sharper edge.

   o **Decontaminate Colors**: This checkbox removes color fringing along the edges of your selection (useful when selecting subjects with colorful backgrounds).

4. **Preview Your Selection**: Use the different view options (such as **On Black**, **On White**, or **Overlay**) to preview how the selection will look against different backgrounds.

5. **Output Settings**: Once satisfied with the selection, choose how you want to output it (e.g., a new layer with a mask or a new layer). Click **OK** to apply the selection.

Refining your selection edges with **Refine Edge** ensures that even complex elements like hair or soft edges are selected with high precision, allowing for more seamless composites and edits.

Quick Mask: A Powerful Tool for Precision

The Quick Mask function in Photoshop allows you to work immediately on your selection as if it were a painting process. This method gives flexibility and accuracy, enabling you to swiftly alter and refine sections that require specific work. Unlike traditional selection methods, Quick Mask allows you to "paint" over your selection with the Brush Tool, giving you precise control over the edges.

How to Use Quick Mask:

1. **Activate Quick Mask**: Press **Q** on your keyboard, or click the **Quick Mask** button at the bottom of the **Tools Panel** to switch to Quick Mask mode. You'll see a red overlay on the areas that are not selected.

2. **Use the Brush Tool**: With Quick Mask mode active, use the **Brush Tool** to paint over the areas you want to select. Painting with **black** will add to the selection, while painting with **white** will subtract from it. You can adjust the brush size and hardness in the **Options Bar** for more precise control.

3. **Refine the Selection**: Once you've painted over the desired areas, press **Q** again to exit Quick Mask mode. Photoshop will convert your painted area into a selection.

4. **Fine-tune with Select and Mask**: After using Quick Mask, you can fine-tune the selection using the **Select and Mask** workspace, as described earlier.

Quick Mask gives you a flexible, hands-on way to refine selections, especially for areas that require more artistic or detailed work, like intricate edges or complex shapes.

Layer Styles and Effects

Layer styles and effects are crucial components in Photoshop that allow you to enhance your layers with a number of visual upgrades, such as shadows, glows, gradients, and more. By applying these styles, you can lend depth, dimension, and visual appeal to your work without permanently modifying the source image or layer. In this section, we'll study how to use Layer Styles and apply effects to your layers to create eye-catching designs.

What Are Layer Styles?

A Layer Style is a set of effects that are applied to a layer. These styles allow you to add several effects, such as shadows, glows, and gradients, to any layer. The beauty of Layer Styles is that they are non-destructive—meaning you may modify or remove them at any time without damaging the underlying picture or layer.

How to Apply Layer Styles:

1. **Select a Layer**: Click on the layer in the **Layers Panel** that you want to apply the style to.

2. **Open the Layer Style Menu**: Right-click on the layer and choose **Blending Options**, or click the **fx** button at the bottom of the Layers Panel.

3. **Choose an Effect**: From the **Layer Style** menu, you can apply a variety of effects:

   ○ **Drop Shadow**: Adds a shadow behind your layer, giving it depth.

   ○ **Inner Shadow**: Adds a shadow inside the layer, creating a recessed effect.

   ○ **Outer Glow**: Adds a soft, glowing edge to the layer.

- **Gradient Overlay**: Applies a gradient effect over your layer, allowing you to create smooth color transitions.

- **Stroke**: Adds an outline around your layer, which can be solid, gradient, or pattern-based.

- **Bevel and Emboss**: Creates a 3D effect by simulating light and shadow on the layer's edges.

4. **Adjust Settings**: Use the sliders and settings within each effect to adjust the intensity, size, angle, and other properties of the effect.

5. **Preview and Apply**: Click **OK** to apply the effects. You'll see them applied directly to the layer in your image.

Layer Styles can be stacked, meaning you can apply numerous effects to a single layer for sophisticated, visually dynamic results. They are very handy for creating polished effects to text, buttons, and design components in your artwork.

Using Effects to Enhance Your Designs

Layer Styles can be utilized creatively to enhance the visual attractiveness of your projects. For example, while developing a website button, you might add a gradient fill with a minor bevel and emboss to make it appear as if the button is raised. Similarly, applying a drop shadow to text can give it a three-dimensional aspect, making it stand out against a background.

Understanding Blending Modes and Their Applications

Blending modes are one of the most effective tools in Photoshop for regulating how layers interact with one another. By employing multiple blending modes, you can modify how the colors and tones of one layer blend with the layer(s) beneath it, resulting in a broad range of visual effects.

What Are Blending Modes?

A Blending Mode regulates how the pixels of one layer blend with the pixels of the layer underneath it. Photoshop offers a range of blending modes that produce distinct effects based on the relationship between colors, brightness, and contrast. The most frequent blending modes are separated into categories, such as Normal, Darken, Lighten, Contrast, and Color.

Common Blending Modes and Their Uses:

1. **Normal**: This is the default blending mode, where the top layer covers the bottom layer completely.

2. **Multiply**: This mode multiplies the base color by the blend color, resulting in a darker color. It's useful for adding shadows or darkening images.

3. **Screen**: The inverse of Multiply, Screen brightens the image by blending the top layer with the base layer, resulting in lighter colors. It's often used for lightening and adding highlights.

4. **Overlay**: This mode combines Multiply and Screen to enhance contrast. It's commonly used for adding depth or texture.

5. **Soft Light**: This mode adds subtle contrast to the image, creating a soft light effect. It's great for enhancing texture or giving images a softer, more natural feel.

6. **Hard Light**: Similar to Overlay, but with a stronger contrast effect, Hard Light can create dramatic lighting effects.

7. **Color**: This mode blends the hue and saturation of the blend layer with the luminosity of the base layer. It's useful for changing colors without affecting brightness.

How to Apply Blending Modes:

1. **Select the Layer**: Click on the layer you want to apply the blending mode to.

2. **Choose a Blending Mode**: In the **Layers Panel**, locate the dropdown menu at the top that says **Normal**. Click the dropdown menu to reveal the list of blending modes.

3. **Preview the Effect**: As you cycle through the blending modes, you'll see the effect applied in real-time. Choose the mode that best fits your desired outcome.

Blending modes are essential for creating special effects, manipulating colors, and working with textures. They're often used in photo manipulation, compositing, and digital painting to create complex effects without the need for additional layers.

Practical Project: Correcting a Portrait Photo

Now that we've covered some of the advanced techniques in Photoshop, let's apply these concepts to a practical project. In this section, we'll walk through the steps to **correct a portrait photo**, using the tools and methods we've discussed in this chapter.

Step 1: Import the Photo and Assess the Image

Open the portrait photo in Photoshop. Begin by analyzing the image and identifying areas that require retouching. Common issues with portraits include:

- **Blemishes** or imperfections on the skin.

- **Uneven lighting** or harsh shadows.

- **Distracting background elements** that need to be removed or blurred.

Step 2: Retouching the Skin

Start by using the **Healing Brush Tool** to remove small blemishes. Paint over the imperfections, allowing Photoshop to sample from nearby areas and blend the textures seamlessly.

Next, use the **Clone Stamp Tool** for larger imperfections, such as scars or uneven skin tones. Be sure to sample from areas that match the surrounding skin tones.

Step 3: Refining the Selection with Quick Mask

To adjust the edges of the subject's hair or refine areas like the eyes or mouth, use **Quick Mask**. This tool allows you to paint over the selection to add or remove areas with precision. Once satisfied, exit Quick Mask and adjust the edges using the **Refine Edge** function.

Step 4: Adjusting the Lighting

To brighten the subject's face and soften any harsh shadows, use an **Adjustment Layer** for **Brightness/Contrast** or **Curves**. You can apply the adjustment to specific areas of the image using a **Layer Mask** to control the regions that need enhancing.

Step 5: Applying Blending Modes and Layer Styles

To add depth to the image, apply a **Soft Light** blending mode to an additional layer. Add a subtle **Drop Shadow** or **Outer Glow** to the subject's hair or clothing using **Layer Styles**.

Step 6: Finalizing the Image

After retouching and making necessary adjustments, fine-tune the image with **Smart Filters** or **Layer Masks** to ensure a seamless, non-destructive workflow. You can also apply a **Gaussian Blur** to the background to create depth and focus on the subject.

Step 7: Save Your Work

Save the image as a **PSD file** to retain all your layers and adjustments. For sharing or printing, export the final image as a **JPEG** or **PNG** for optimized file sizes and quality.

In this chapter, we've covered advanced Photoshop techniques, including Refine Edge and Quick Mask for precise selections, Layer Styles and Blending Modes for generating dynamic effects, and we've finished a practical project where we employed these techniques to repair a portrait photo.

These strategies not only increase your creative process but also provide you the ability to make professional-level edits to your photographs.

Mastering these techniques will boost your Photoshop skills and allow you to face a wide range of editing tasks, from portrait retouching to complicated compositing.

Chapter 4

Advanced Image Manipulation – Creative Control and Precision

Adobe Photoshop 2025 continues to be the industry leader in digital editing, offering powerful capabilities for both novices and seasoned pros. However, to fully unlock Photoshop's potential, it's vital to progress beyond basic picture alterations and dive into the advanced capabilities that offer the precision and versatility required for professional-grade work. In this chapter, we'll focus on techniques that allow creative control over your photographs with a high degree of precision.

While basic adjustments might improve an image, advanced image manipulation techniques allow you to modify, polish, and manipulate every aspect inside a composition. This chapter covers advanced masks, layer compositions, advanced selects, and digital painting techniques. Whether you're working with precise selections, fine-tuning details, or producing bespoke artwork from scratch, these tools and approaches will allow you the freedom and flexibility to take your creativity to the next level.

Working with Advanced Masks and Layer Compositions

Masks are one of the most powerful features in Photoshop because they allow you to edit certain sections of an image without altering the original pixel data. Advanced masks and layer compositions take this notion even further, enabling more flexibility and precision for complicated editing jobs. Whether you're building multi-layered compositions or refining fine details, learning masks and layers will make your work more versatile and efficient.

Advanced Layer Masks

A Layer Mask allows you to hide or show areas of a layer without destroying any pixel data. By painting on the mask with black, you hide parts of the layer, while painting with white shows it. Grayscale shades of gray allow for partial transparency, producing gentle transitions.

However, when your compositions get more sophisticated, working with conventional masks may not be adequate. Advanced Layer Masks involve techniques like color-based masking, gradient masks, and enhanced edge masks to make your selections more exact.

How to Create and Use Advanced Layer Masks:

1. **Basic Masking**: Begin with a simple **Layer Mask** by selecting a layer and clicking the **Add Layer Mask** button at the bottom of the Layers Panel. The mask will appear as a thumbnail next to your layer. Use the **Brush Tool** to paint black or white on the mask to hide or reveal portions of the layer.

2. **Color-Based Masking**: You can create masks based on color ranges in your image by using **Select > Color Range**. This is especially useful for isolating specific colors in an image, like the blue in a sky or green in foliage.

3. **Gradient Masks**: Apply a **gradient** to your mask to create smooth transitions between visible and hidden areas. This is useful when you want to apply effects like gradual fades or selective focus.

4. **Refining Mask Edges**: When working with selections involving fine details like hair or fur, use the **Select and Mask** workspace to refine your edges. In this workspace, you can smooth, feather, and refine selections with a variety of brushes and tools.

By mastering these advanced masking techniques, you can create seamless composites, remove backgrounds with ease, and control every detail of your image.

Layer Compositions: Building Complex Images

Layer compositions involve stacking multiple layers to create a complete image, each layer serving a specific function. For example, in a composite image, one layer might contain the background, while another holds the subject, and another contains textures or effects.

How to Work with Layer Compositions:

1. **Organize Layers**: Use the **Layers Panel** to organize and label your layers. Group related layers by selecting multiple layers and pressing **Ctrl + G** (Windows) or **Cmd + G** (Mac) to create a group.

2. **Layer Masking in Compositions**: Apply **layer masks** to individual layers to control which parts of the layer are visible. For example, if you have a layer of text over a background, you can apply a mask to gradually fade the text in or out.

3. **Adjustment Layers**: Use **Adjustment Layers** to apply global effects (such as color corrections or contrast adjustments) to an entire group of layers without affecting the original content.

4. **Smart Objects in Compositions**: Convert your layers into **Smart Objects** to apply non-destructive filters and transformations. Smart Objects preserve the original content, allowing you to resize and transform without losing quality.

By mastering layer compositions and using advanced masking techniques, you can create intricate and dynamic compositions that are easy to manage and edit.

Advanced Selections: Magic Wand, Pen Tool, and Calculations

Selections are the backbone of many Photoshop adjustments. Whether you're isolating a subject, removing a background, or applying selective modifications, advanced selection techniques are necessary for precision. Photoshop includes various tools and methods to make selections, but the Magic Wand, Pen Tool, and Calculations provide additional features that take your selections to the next level.

Magic Wand Tool: Selecting by Color

The Magic Wand Tool (W) is one of the fastest ways to make selections based on color. It operates by picking all pixels of a similar color inside a specific area. This tool is great for creating rapid selections of solid-colored areas or isolating subjects with distinct color variances from the background.

How to Use the Magic Wand Tool:

1. Select the **Magic Wand Tool** from the **Tools Panel** or press **W** on your keyboard.

2. Click on an area of your image that you want to select. The Magic Wand will select all connected pixels that are similar in color.

3. Adjust the **Tolerance** in the **Options Bar** to increase or decrease the range of colors selected. A higher tolerance selects a broader range of similar colors.

4. Use the **Add to Selection** or **Subtract from Selection** options in the Options Bar to expand or refine your selection.

While the **Magic Wand** is excellent for selecting large, uniform areas, its accuracy can suffer in areas with subtle gradients or fine details. This is where the **Pen Tool** comes in.

Pen Tool: Precision Selections

The **Pen Tool** (P) is the gold standard for making **precise, editable selections**. Unlike other selection tools, the **Pen Tool** creates paths that can be converted into selections. The **Pen Tool** is particularly useful when you need to make selections with sharp curves, straight lines, or angular edges, such as selecting a subject's silhouette or creating complex paths.

How to Use the Pen Tool:

1. Select the **Pen Tool** from the **Tools Panel** or press **P** on your keyboard.

2. Click to create **anchor points** along the edges of the object you want to select. Hold and drag the anchor points to create curves.

3. After completing the path, close it by clicking on the first anchor point. Right-click and choose **Make Selection** to convert the path into a selection.

4. Refine the selection as needed using the **Select and Mask** workspace for smooth, natural edges.

The **Pen Tool** is the most accurate and flexible tool for creating complex, clean selections, and it's a crucial tool for advanced compositing and photo manipulation.

Calculations: Advanced Selections Based on Channels

For highly specific selections, the **Calculations** command in Photoshop allows you to combine and manipulate the color channels (Red, Green, and Blue) of an image to create selections based on color and contrast. This method is particularly useful when working with images that have complex color variations or when you need to extract fine details from the image.

How to Use Calculations for Advanced Selections:

1. Go to **Image > Calculations**.

2. In the **Calculations** dialog box, select two color channels to combine. Photoshop will create a new channel based on the combination of these channels.

3. Use the **Blend** mode and **Opacity** sliders to fine-tune the selection. Once satisfied with the results, click **OK**.

4. Convert the resulting channel into a selection by **Ctrl-clicking** (Windows) or **Cmd-clicking** (Mac) on the channel thumbnail in the Channels Panel.

Using **Calculations** allows you to create highly precise selections based on the tonal or color information in the image. This technique is especially useful for high-end compositing or extracting fine details that would be difficult to isolate with other selection methods.

Digital Painting Techniques: Brush Settings and Pressure Sensitivity

Digital painting in Photoshop has become a vital ability for painters, illustrators, and designers. The Brush Tool is one of the most versatile tools for painting in Photoshop, allowing you to create everything from soft, blended textures to crisp, defined strokes. Mastering brush settings and pressure sensitivity will allow you the ability to create realistic, dynamic brush strokes with precision.

Brush Settings: Customizing Your Brushes for Different Effects

The Brush Tool allows you to alter many settings to fit your painting style. Whether you're producing complex artwork or applying textures, changing your brush settings is vital for attaining the desired impact.

How to Customize Brush Settings:

1. Select the **Brush Tool** from the **Tools Panel** or press **B** on your keyboard.

2. Open the **Brush Settings Panel** by going to **Window > Brush Settings**.

3. Adjust the following settings:

   o **Size**: Controls the diameter of the brush. Use the [and] keys to quickly change the size while painting.

   o **Hardness**: Determines the edge softness of the brush. A higher hardness creates sharp edges, while a lower hardness creates softer, feathered edges.

   o **Spacing**: Controls how frequently the brush marks are placed along the stroke.

   o **Shape Dynamics**: Adjusts properties such as **angle**, **roundness**, and **size jitter** to create variation in your strokes.

   o **Texture**: Adds texture to the brush stroke by applying patterns or images.

- **Dual Brush**: Combines two brushes for more complex effects, such as textured strokes with different brush dynamics.

Experiment with different brush settings to create a wide variety of painting effects, from soft gradients to hard, defined edges.

Pressure Sensitivity: Working with Drawing Tablets

If you're working with a **drawing tablet** (such as a Wacom tablet), Photoshop's pressure sensitivity allows you to control the opacity, flow, and size of your brush strokes based on how hard you press. This gives you the ability to create more natural, expressive strokes, similar to traditional painting.

How to Use Pressure Sensitivity:

1. Ensure that **Shape Dynamics** is enabled in the **Brush Settings Panel**.

2. In the **Size Jitter** and **Control** options, select **Pen Pressure** to control the size of the brush based on pressure.

3. Similarly, you can adjust the **Opacity Jitter** and **Flow Jitter** to respond to pressure, allowing for variable opacity and flow as you paint.

Using pressure sensitivity allows you to mimic the feel of traditional brushes, giving you more control and flexibility in your digital artwork.

High-End Retouching: Frequency Separation and Dodge & Burn

When it comes to high-end retouching, obtaining a smooth and natural look without over-editing is a difficult balance. Two of the most potent techniques employed by expert retouchers are frequency separation and dodge and burn. These techniques let you work on the texture and color of an image individually, retaining the natural feel while addressing errors.

Frequency Separation: Dividing Texture and Color

Frequency Separation is a technique that separates the high frequency (fine features and textures) from the low frequency (colors and tones) in a picture. By doing this, you may modify the skin tone, shadows, and highlights without changing the texture, and vice versa.

How to Perform Frequency Separation:

1. **Duplicate the Background Layer**: Begin by duplicating the **Background Layer** twice. The first duplicate will be used for the low-frequency layer (color), and the second duplicate will be used for the high-frequency layer (texture).

2. **Apply Gaussian Blur to the Low-Frequency Layer**: On the first duplicate layer, go to **Filter > Blur > Gaussian Blur**. Set the radius to blur out the fine details and smooth the colors. The amount of blur should be enough to make the details in the image soft and blurred, but not so much that you lose the overall shape of the subject.

3. **Apply High Pass Filter to the High-Frequency Layer**: Select the second duplicate layer and convert it to a **Smart Object**. Then, go to **Filter > Other > High Pass** and apply a radius that reveals the fine details. The high pass filter sharpens the image and brings back the texture you need for retouching.

4. **Combine the Layers**: Set the blending mode of the high-frequency layer to **Linear Light**. This will combine the low-frequency and high-frequency layers, creating an image that retains its texture while giving you full control over the color and tonality.

5. **Retouch the Low-Frequency Layer**: Use the **Clone Stamp** or **Healing Brush Tool** on the low-frequency layer to adjust the skin tone or fix color imbalances without affecting the texture.

6. **Retouch the High-Frequency Layer**: Use the **Spot Healing Brush Tool** or **Clone Stamp Tool** on the high-frequency layer to smooth out skin textures or remove blemishes, leaving the skin looking natural.

The beauty of **frequency separation** lies in its ability to give you control over both the skin tone and the texture separately, ensuring that your retouching looks realistic and subtle.

Dodge and Burn: Sculpting Light and Shadow

The **Dodge and Burn** technique is used to lighten (dodge) or darken (burn) specific areas of your image, helping to enhance highlights, shadows, and overall depth. This technique is essential for sculpting the light and adding dimension to portraits, giving your image a more dramatic, three-dimensional feel.

How to Apply Dodge and Burn:

1. **Create a New Layer**: To dodge and burn non-destructively, create a **new empty layer** and set its blending mode to **Overlay**. Then, fill the layer with 50% gray by going to **Edit > Fill** and choosing **50% Gray**.

2. **Dodge (Lighten)**: Select the **Dodge Tool** (O) from the **Tools Panel** and set the range to **Midtones**. Use a low exposure setting (5-10%) and gently paint over the areas you want to lighten, such as the highlights on the cheekbones, nose, and forehead.

3. **Burn (Darken)**: Select the **Burn Tool** (O) and set the range to **Midtones** as well. Use a low exposure setting (5-10%) and paint over the shadowed areas of the image to add depth and contrast.

4. **Refine Your Work**: Toggle the visibility of the **Dodge and Burn** layer to compare the before and after effect. Adjust the opacity of the layer if necessary to control the intensity of the effect.

Dodge and burn is a fantastic way to add dimension to your images, sculpting light and shadow for a more dynamic and artistic look.

Working with Filters: Camera Raw, Gaussian Blur, and Lens Effects

Photoshop's **filter tools** are a fantastic way to enhance your image with special effects, texture, or fine-tuned adjustments. Filters allow you to add a variety of effects, from subtle adjustments to dramatic changes. Here, we'll look at three essential filters for high-end editing: **Camera Raw**, **Gaussian Blur**, and **Lens Effects**.

Camera Raw Filter: Enhancing Exposure and Color

The **Camera Raw Filter** is one of Photoshop's most powerful tools, especially when working with raw image files. Even if you're working with JPEGs or TIFFs, the Camera Raw filter provides precise control over exposure, color, and sharpness.

How to Use the Camera Raw Filter:

1. **Convert to Smart Object**: First, convert your image to a **Smart Object** to preserve the editability of the Camera Raw filter.

2. **Apply the Camera Raw Filter**: Go to **Filter > Camera Raw Filter** to open the Camera Raw dialog box.

3. **Adjust Basic Settings**: Use the **Basic Panel** to adjust exposure, contrast, highlights, shadows, whites, and blacks. You can also adjust the **White Balance** for more accurate colors.

4. **Enhance Details**: The **Detail Panel** lets you fine-tune the sharpness and reduce noise in your image. The **Noise Reduction** sliders are particularly useful for cleaning up images that were shot at high ISO.

5. **Use the HSL/Grayscale Panel**: This panel allows you to adjust the **hue**, **saturation**, and **luminance** of individual colors in the image, making it easy to isolate and enhance certain color ranges.

The **Camera Raw Filter** is essential for giving your image a polished, professional finish, especially for color correction and exposure adjustments.

Gaussian Blur: Softening and Smoothing

The **Gaussian Blur** filter is often used to soften an image or create a smooth, blurred effect. It's especially useful for smoothing out harsh textures, removing noise, or creating a **depth-of-field** effect.

How to Use Gaussian Blur:

1. **Apply the Gaussian Blur**: Go to **Filter > Blur > Gaussian Blur**. In the dialog box, adjust the radius slider to control the intensity of the blur.

2. **Use for Backgrounds**: If you're working with portraits, apply **Gaussian Blur** to the background to create a bokeh effect, helping to draw attention to the subject.

Using **Gaussian Blur** can transform a harsh, busy background into a soft, pleasing backdrop that doesn't distract from the main subject.

Lens Effects: Adding Depth and Focus

The **Lens Effects** filter is often used to simulate the effects of a real camera lens. It can be used to add bokeh, vignette, or even simulate the lens flare effect, making your images feel more dynamic and cinematic.

How to Use Lens Effects:

1. **Apply the Lens Effect**: Go to **Filter > Lens Correction**, and in the dialog box, select the **Custom** tab.

2. **Vignette**: Use the vignette controls to darken the corners of the image and draw focus toward the center.

3. **Bokeh Effects**: The **Bokeh** option allows you to create out-of-focus light spots that add a creative blur to the image, simulating the effect of a shallow depth of field.

The **Lens Effects** filter can be used creatively to add cinematic effects, enhance focus, and manipulate the overall mood of your image.

Manipulating Light and Shadows: Creating Depth and Contrast

Manipulating light and shadows is vital to generating a sense of depth and contrast in your photos. By altering the lighting, you can guide the viewer's eye and highlight essential components in your picture. This approach is particularly beneficial for creating dramatic, high-impact photos, such as portraits and product photography.

How to Manipulate Light and Shadows:

1. **Use Dodging and Burning**: As we discussed earlier, **dodge and burn** can enhance the highlights and shadows, adding dimension to your image. Focus on lighting the high points (like cheekbones, the nose, or shoulders) and darkening the shadowed areas (like under the chin or around the eyes).

2. **Apply a Vignette**: A vignette can be added to darken the edges of the image, forcing the viewer's attention toward the center. Use **Lens Effects** or the **Gradient Tool** with a soft, black gradient to create a subtle vignette effect.

3. **Enhance Contrast**: Increase contrast using **Curves** or **Levels** to make shadows darker and highlights brighter. This will help to create more dynamic lighting in your image, enhancing depth and interest.

4. **Use Lighting Filters**: Photoshop's **Lighting Effects** filter (found under **Filter > Render > Lighting Effects**) allows you to add spotlights, point lights, and other light sources. Experiment with different lighting positions to create dramatic lighting setups.

By carefully manipulating light and shadows, you can transform flat images into dynamic, three-dimensional works of art that draw the viewer's eye.

Project: Creating a Dramatic Portrait Using Advanced Retouching

Now that we've covered the key advanced techniques, it's time to apply them in a practical project. Let's create a **dramatic portrait** using the tools and techniques we've discussed.

Step 1: Import the Image and Analyze the Subject

Start by opening a high-quality portrait in Photoshop. Examine the image to identify areas that could benefit from retouching, such as uneven skin tones, harsh lighting, or distracting background elements. Also, assess the light and shadows in the image to determine if adjustments are needed to enhance the depth and contrast.

Step 2: Frequency Separation

Apply **frequency separation** to separate the texture from the color and smooth out skin tones. Use the **Healing Brush Tool** to fix blemishes and the **Clone Stamp Tool** for more detailed corrections on the high-frequency layer. Be sure to maintain natural skin texture while adjusting the tone and color in the low-frequency layer.

Step 3: Dodge and Burn for Dimension

Use the **Dodge and Burn** technique to enhance the light and shadows on the subject's face. Lighten the high points of the face, such as the forehead, cheekbones, and nose, and darken the areas under the chin, neck, and eyes for added depth.

Step 4: Apply Gaussian Blur to Background

To emphasize the subject, apply a **Gaussian Blur** to the background, creating a bokeh effect. This will help draw attention to the subject's face while softening any distractions in the background.

Step 5: Manipulate Light with Lens Effects

Add a subtle **vignette** effect to the image using the **Lens Effects** filter. This will create a natural focus on the subject's face and add a sense of depth to the portrait.

Step 6: Final Touches

Finally, make any additional color or lighting adjustments using the **Camera Raw Filter**. Fine-tune the exposure, contrast, and sharpness to ensure the portrait has the desired dramatic effect.

Step 7: Save and Export

Save the edited portrait as a **PSD** to preserve the layers and editing history. For sharing or printing, export the image as a **JPEG** or **PNG**.

Now, we've covered advanced approaches in picture manipulation, focusing on high-end retouching, precise filter effects, and the manipulation of light and shadows. These techniques provide you creative flexibility and allow you to generate professional-quality edits with better precision.

Chapter 5

Working with Vectors and Paths - Drawing and Illustration in Photoshop

Adobe Photoshop is widely known for its raster-based editing capabilities, allowing users to manipulate pixels and produce attractive images with fine details. However, Photoshop also features strong vector tools that enable designers and illustrators to produce scalable images, tidy paths, and complicated designs without losing quality. This chapter is dedicated to studying the integration of vectors and paths in Photoshop, providing you the ability to broaden your creative potential.

Unlike raster graphics, which are pixel-based, vectors are defined by mathematical equations and are resolution-independent, meaning they may be enlarged infinitely without losing detail or clarity. Whether you're designing logos, producing illustrations, or drawing complex objects, vectors in Photoshop give you control over smooth lines, curves, and perfectly aligned shapes, making it easier to make high-quality graphics for print or web use.

In this chapter, we will introduce you to working with vectors and paths in Photoshop, starting with the Pen Tool for producing straight lines and curves, followed by techniques for creating and altering shapes—from simple geometric forms to intricate, unique designs. By the end of this chapter, you will have a good grasp of how to include vector sketching and editing into your Photoshop workflow, allowing you to enhance your designs with accuracy and flexibility.

Vectors and Paths in Photoshop

In Photoshop, vectors are used to produce forms, lines, and paths that may be modified and scaled without affecting their quality. While Photoshop is usually recognized for its pixel-based, raster editing, the presence of vector tools allows you to create scalable artwork, logos, icons, and complex illustrations that can be enlarged without losing resolution.

What Are Vectors?

Vectors are graphics formed using pathways, which are specified by a start point, end point, and other points in between. The fundamental advantage of vector graphics is that they are resolution-independent. Unlike pixel-based images, which can become fuzzy or pixelated when scaled, vector graphics keep their clarity regardless of how large or tiny you make them.

Vectors are constructed using mathematical formulas that determine lines, curves, and forms. This makes them excellent for generating logos, infographics, icons, and other artwork that needs to be used in numerous sizes.

Paths in Photoshop

A route in Photoshop is a line or shape that is formed by anchor points connected by segments (either straight or curved). Paths are used to define vector-based forms and lines. They can be produced and modified with the Pen Tool and can be transformed into selections, used to construct vector shapes, or filled with color.

There are two types of paths in Photoshop:

- **Work Paths**: Temporary paths that are not saved with the image unless you choose to save them.

- **Shape Layers**: Paths that are filled with color or a gradient, forming a shape layer. These paths are used for creating vector shapes.

Working with paths in Photoshop allows for precise control over the form, position, and curvature of your artwork. You can adjust the curves, angles, and even the smoothness of lines to create intricate designs.

Why Use Vectors and Paths in Photoshop?

- **Scalability**: Vectors can be resized infinitely without loss of quality, making them ideal for designs that need to be used at different sizes (e.g., logos or icons).

- **Precision**: Paths provide a high level of precision when drawing and editing lines and curves, making it easier to create clean, professional-looking designs.

- **Non-Destructive Editing**: Since vector paths are separate from the pixel-based layers, you can manipulate and adjust them without affecting the rest of your image.

- **Integration with Other Adobe Apps**: Vector elements created in Photoshop can be easily imported into other Adobe Creative Cloud apps, such as Illustrator and InDesign, to create a cohesive design workflow.

Using the Pen Tool: Creating Curves and Straight Lines

The Pen Tool is one of the most powerful vector tools in Photoshop. It allows you to create paths that form shapes, lines, and intricate drawings. Whether you're sketching fine details, making logos, or carving precise curves, the Pen Tool gives the accuracy and versatility you need for professional-quality artwork.

Pen Tool Basics

The Pen Tool (P) can generate straight lines, curved lines, and combinations of both. It works by putting anchor points at certain locations and defining pathways between those sites. The line linking the anchor points is termed a path.

Creating Straight Lines:

1. Select the **Pen Tool** from the **Tools Panel** or press **P** on your keyboard.

2. Click on the canvas to place the first anchor point. Click again where you want the straight line to end. Photoshop will automatically create a straight line between the two points.

3. Continue clicking to create additional straight segments. To finish, either click on the first anchor point or press **Ctrl + Enter** (Windows) or **Cmd + Enter** (Mac) to finalize the path.

Creating Curved Lines:

To create curves with the Pen Tool, click and **drag** the anchor points instead of just clicking. Dragging will create **direction handles**, which control the curve's shape.

1. Select the **Pen Tool** and click to place the first anchor point.

2. Click and drag the second anchor point. The longer you drag, the more pronounced the curve will be.

3. Continue adding anchor points, clicking and dragging to adjust the direction handles and create smooth curves.

4. To adjust the curve later, use the **Direct Selection Tool** (A) to modify the direction handles of each anchor point.

Working with Anchor Points and Direction Handles

- **Anchor Points**: These are the points where the path begins or changes direction. When you click with the Pen Tool, you create an anchor point.

- **Direction Handles**: When you click and drag an anchor point, direction handles appear. These handles define the direction of the curve and its curvature. The longer the handles, the sharper the curve.

- **Adjusting Curves**: After creating a curve, you can adjust its shape by selecting the anchor point with the **Direct Selection Tool** and dragging the direction handles. This lets you modify the curvature of a line without affecting other parts of the path.

Creating Complex Paths

To make complicated forms and graphics, employ a combination of straight lines and curves. You may connect anchor points and utilize direction handles to construct complicated shapes. The Pen Tool allows you full control over the shape and form of your paths, making it excellent for producing logos, complex illustrations, and vector-based artwork.

Converting Paths into Selections

Once you've created a path with the Pen Tool, you can convert it into a selection. To do this:

1. Right-click on the path and choose **Make Selection**.

2. You'll be prompted to adjust the feathering and other selection settings before applying the selection.

Paths created with the Pen Tool can also be filled with color, patterns, or gradients, giving you endless possibilities for creating shapes, illustrations, and intricate designs.

Creating and Editing Shapes: From Simple to Complex

Creating forms is a vital facet of design work, whether you're developing icons, logos, or even digital art. Photoshop has a variety of shape tools that allow you to design basic and sophisticated shapes with ease. You can build shapes directly or use the Pen Tool to create bespoke designs.

Using the Shape Tools

Photoshop offers various predefined Shape Tools that allow you to make rectangles, ellipses, polygons, and lines. These forms are vector-based, meaning they can be enlarged without sacrificing quality.

How to Create Simple Shapes:

1. Select the **Shape Tool** from the **Tools Panel**.

2. Choose the shape you want to create (e.g., Rectangle, Ellipse, Polygon).

3. Click and drag on the canvas to draw the shape. Hold down **Shift** while dragging to constrain the proportions (e.g., to create a perfect square or circle).

4. Use the **Options Bar** to adjust the shape's fill color, stroke color, and other properties.

Shapes can be filled with color or gradients, and you can adjust their size, position, and alignment.

Creating Custom Shapes with the Pen Tool

For more complex designs, the **Pen Tool** allows you to create custom vector shapes. Whether you're drawing intricate logos, abstract designs, or freeform illustrations, the **Pen Tool** gives you the flexibility to create complex paths and convert them into shapes.

Editing Shapes with the Direct Selection Tool:

1. Select the **Direct Selection Tool** (A) from the **Tools Panel**.

2. Click on the path or anchor point of the shape you want to modify.

3. You can move the anchor points, adjust direction handles, or change the shape's properties.

Combining and Modifying Shapes

Photoshop allows you to combine multiple shapes into a single design using the **Shape Path Operations**. You can add, subtract, or intersect shapes to create complex designs.

How to Combine Shapes:

1. Create multiple shapes using the **Shape Tool** or **Pen Tool**.

2. In the **Paths Panel**, select the paths you want to combine.

3. Choose an operation from the **Options Bar**:

   ○ **Unite**: Combines shapes into one.

   ○ **Subtract**: Removes the top shape from the bottom shape.

   ○ **Intersect**: Creates a shape from the overlapping areas of the selected shapes.

   ○ **Exclude**: Removes the overlapping areas, leaving only the non-overlapping parts.

These operations give you the ability to create complex designs with precision and ease.

Using the PathFinder and Shape Builder

For more advanced shape manipulation, you can use the **Path Finder** (in Illustrator) or **Shape Builder** tool (found in the **Path Operations** section). These tools allow you to subtract, combine, or intersect multiple paths or shapes, offering more control over your design.

Combining Paths: Shape Builder Tool and Pathfinder Techniques

One of the primary advantages of working with vectors in Photoshop is the ability to combine and edit paths in precise and powerful ways. Combining pathways allows you to construct more complicated and dynamic shapes from simple geometric parts. Photoshop's Shape Builder Tool and Pathfinder Techniques provide you the ability to do these jobs with flexibility and ease.

The Shape Builder Tool: A Powerful Way to Combine and Modify Paths

The Shape Builder Tool is a relatively new addition to Photoshop that allows you to work easily with vector shapes by merging, removing, or changing pathways directly on your canvas. Instead of depending on standard selection methods, the Shape Builder Tool enables you to draw directly on the routes to combine or divide them. This provides a simpler and more artistic technique to construct complex forms.

How to Use the Shape Builder Tool:

1. **Create Basic Shapes**: Start by creating basic vector shapes, such as a rectangle, ellipse, or polygon, using the **Shape Tool**.

2. **Activate the Shape Builder Tool**: Select the **Shape Builder Tool** from the **Tools Panel** or press **Shift + M**. The cursor will change to a shape builder icon, indicating that you're ready to work on your paths.

3. **Combine Paths**: Hold down the **Alt** (Windows) or **Option** (Mac) key, then click on the areas of the shapes you want to combine. The tool will merge the paths into one shape. You can continue building your design by adding or subtracting paths.

4. **Subtract Paths**: To subtract a section of a shape, simply click on the area you want to remove while holding the **Alt** (Windows) or **Option** (Mac) key.

5. **Refine Shapes**: After building your desired shape, you can refine the design by adjusting anchor points or using the **Direct Selection Tool** (A) to fine-tune the curves and angles.

The **Shape Builder Tool** offers a hands-on, intuitive method for combining multiple shapes or subtracting sections, making it ideal for complex designs that require quick and creative adjustments.

Pathfinder Techniques: Advanced Path Operations

Photoshop also offers powerful **Pathfinder techniques**, which are essential for combining, subtracting, and intersecting paths to create complex vector designs. While the **Shape Builder Tool** is more visual, the **Pathfinder** options provide precise control over how paths interact with one another.

Common Pathfinder Operations:

1. **Unite**: Combines two or more paths into a single shape. This is useful when you want to create a unified shape from separate elements.

2. **Subtract**: Removes the top shape from the bottom shape, leaving a hole in the original shape. This is often used to create cutouts or negative space.

3. **Intersect**: Creates a new shape from the overlapping area of two or more paths. This is ideal for creating shapes from intersections.

4. **Exclude**: Removes the overlapping areas between two shapes, leaving only the non-overlapping portions.

How to Use the Pathfinder Panel:

1. **Create Multiple Shapes**: Start by drawing multiple shapes using the **Shape Tool** or **Pen Tool**.

2. **Open the Pathfinder Panel**: Go to **Window > Pathfinder** to open the **Pathfinder Panel**.

3. **Select the Paths**: Use the **Path Selection Tool** (A) to select the paths you want to modify.

4. **Apply the Desired Operation**: In the **Pathfinder Panel**, choose the operation that best suits your design needs. Photoshop will apply the selected path operation to the shapes.

These advanced **Pathfinder techniques** give you the flexibility to combine and modify paths, making them an invaluable part of the design process.

Converting Raster Images to Vectors

One of the most powerful aspects of Photoshop is its ability to turn raster pictures (pixel-based images) into vectors. This approach is essential when dealing with logos, images, or any design that needs to be scaled and changeable without losing quality. Converting raster images to vectors allows you to work with scalable, editable pathways rather than pixels, which makes it easier to change and resize your designs.

Why Convert Raster to Vector?

Converting raster images to vectors offers several key benefits:

- **Scalability**: Vectors are resolution-independent, meaning they can be resized without losing quality.

- **Editability**: Once converted, vectors can be easily edited, allowing you to change shapes, colors, and lines without affecting the overall quality.

- **Clean Lines and Smooth Edges**: Raster images, especially low-resolution ones, often appear pixelated when scaled. Converting them to vectors smooths out edges and ensures clean lines, making your artwork look crisp and professional.

How to Convert Raster Images to Vectors in Photoshop

There are two main methods for converting raster images to vectors in Photoshop: **using the Pen Tool** to manually trace the image or **using the Image Trace feature** (found in Illustrator, but accessible in Photoshop with some limitations).

Method 1: Tracing with the Pen Tool

The most effective way to convert a raster image into a vector in Photoshop is to manually trace it using the **Pen Tool**. This allows for maximum control over the final result.

1. **Open the Raster Image**: Start by opening the raster image you want to convert in Photoshop.

2. **Create a New Layer**: Above the image layer, create a new layer to draw the vector paths on.

3. **Trace with the Pen Tool**: Use the **Pen Tool** (P) to trace over the parts of the image you want to convert. Start by creating paths along the edges of the image. Each click creates anchor points, and dragging the anchor points creates curves.

4. **Refine the Path**: Once you've traced the key elements, use the **Direct Selection Tool** (A) to adjust the curves and angles of the paths for a smooth, clean line.

5. **Fill the Paths**: After you've completed the vector paths, you can use the **Shape Tool** or **Brush Tool** to fill the paths with color or gradients.

6. **Finalize the Vector Artwork**: Once you're satisfied with the vectorized paths, you can delete the original raster image layer, leaving you with a fully vectorized design.

Method 2: Using Image Trace in Illustrator

Although Photoshop doesn't offer an automatic trace feature like Illustrator, you can open a raster image in **Adobe Illustrator** and use its **Image Trace** feature to convert the image to a vector. You can then import the vectorized image back into Photoshop for further editing.

1. **Open the Raster Image in Illustrator**: Open the image in **Adobe Illustrator**.

2. **Use Image Trace**: Select the image and go to **Window > Image Trace**. Choose a preset trace option (e.g., **Black and White Logo** for simple images or **6 Colors** for more detailed designs).

3. **Expand the Image**: Once the image is traced, click **Expand** in the top toolbar to convert the traced image into editable vector paths.

4. **Save and Import into Photoshop**: Save the vector artwork as an **AI** or **SVG** file and import it into Photoshop for further adjustments.

Project: Designing a Simple Logo Using Vectors and Paths

Now that we've covered the theory and tools for working with vectors and paths, let's apply what we've learned to create a **simple logo** using vectors in Photoshop. This practical project will guide you through the process of designing a logo from scratch using vector shapes, paths, and advanced path operations.

Step 1: Brainstorm the Logo Concept

Start by sketching or planning the concept of your logo. Think about the **shape**, **color scheme**, and the **message** you want to convey. A logo should be simple, memorable, and versatile.

For this example, let's create a logo for a fictional brand: **"Luna Cafe"**, a coffee shop with a modern, minimalist aesthetic. The logo will feature a crescent moon and a coffee cup, combining geometric shapes with smooth curves.

Step 2: Create the Basic Shapes

1. **Draw the Crescent Moon**: Select the **Ellipse Tool** to create a perfect circle. Once you have the circle, duplicate the shape and subtract a smaller circle from it using the **Shape Builder Tool**. This will give you a crescent shape.

2. **Create the Coffee Cup**: Use the **Rectangle Tool** to create the base of the cup. Then, use the **Ellipse Tool** to create the top of the cup. Use the **Direct Selection Tool** to adjust the anchor points and refine the shape.

3. **Refine the Logo**: Combine the crescent moon and coffee cup to create a cohesive design. You can adjust the size, position, and rotation of each shape using the **Path Selection Tool** (A).

Step 3: Add Text to the Logo

1. **Select the Text Tool** and type **"Luna Cafe"** below the graphic. Choose a clean, modern font that complements the logo's minimalist style.

2. Adjust the **font size** and **spacing** using the **Character Panel** to ensure the text fits nicely with the graphic.

Step 4: Combine Paths Using the Shape Builder Tool

1. Once you have the shapes and text positioned, use the **Shape Builder Tool** to merge, subtract, or refine the paths to create a unified design. For instance, you can subtract unnecessary shapes or combine the elements of the moon and coffee cup.

Step 5: Add Color and Final Adjustments

1. Apply **fill colors** to your vector shapes using the **Fill** option in the **Options Bar**.

2. If desired, use **Layer Styles** to add effects like a **Drop Shadow** or **Outer Glow** to the text to make it stand out.

Step 6: Save and Export the Logo

Once your logo is complete, save the file as a **PSD** to retain the layers. For scalable output, export the logo as an **SVG** or **AI** file for use in web and print designs.

In this chapter, we've studied the capability of working with vectors and paths in Photoshop. From mixing paths using the Shape Builder Tool and Pathfinder methods to transforming raster pictures into vectors, these sophisticated techniques allow you to create high-quality, scalable visuals with precision. We also completed a practical project, drawing a simple logo from scratch, employing the vector principles we taught.

Mastering vectors and paths is a crucial skill for any designer or illustrator. By combining these strategies into your workflow, you'll be able to make professional logos, drawings, and other vector-based designs with ease. In the next chapter, we'll go deeper into advanced illustration techniques, where we'll study more complicated design aspects and how to edit your artwork for final output.

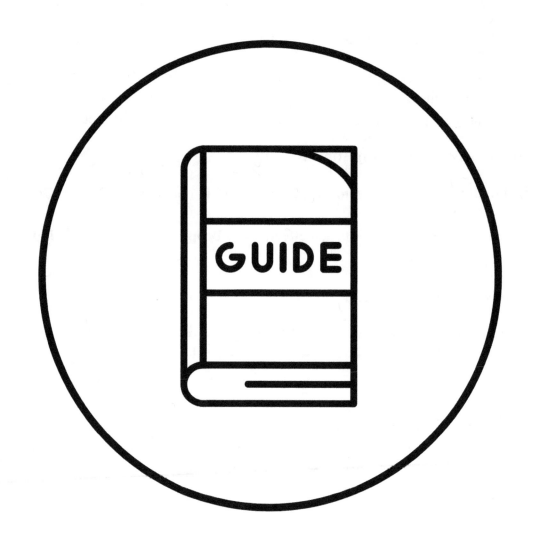

Chapter 6

Photoshop 2025 New Features – What's New in This Version

Adobe Photoshop has long been the industry leader in digital image processing, and with each new edition, Adobe continues to raise the bar for creativity, precision, and usability. With Photoshop 2025, Adobe provides a range of groundbreaking capabilities that streamline processes, enhance creative possibilities, and integrate sophisticated artificial intelligence (AI) tools into the design process. Whether you're a photographer, graphic designer, or digital artist, the 2025 release offers innovations that will greatly boost both your productivity and creative flexibility.

From powerful AI-powered tools like Content-Aware Fill and Neural Filters, to enhanced selection tools and more customizable workspaces, Photoshop 2025 includes a package of capabilities that will make your editing process faster, more intuitive, and more adaptable. The revised user interface (UI) further improves the overall experience, making Photoshop even more user-friendly and accessible, regardless of your ability level.

In this chapter, we will cover the most intriguing new features in Photoshop 2025, starting with the AI-powered tools that promise to revolutionize how you edit your photographs. We'll then go into the improved selection tools that offer better accuracy and efficiency for difficult editing jobs. Finally, we'll examine the adjustable workspaces and the new UI modifications that make Photoshop even more versatile and user-friendly for your unique needs.

New AI-Powered Features: Content-Aware Fill and Neural Filters

One of the most notable advancements in Photoshop 2025 is the inclusion of artificial intelligence (AI) features that enable for faster and more intelligent editing. Adobe's effort to upgrade Photoshop with AI-driven capabilities has brought tools like Content-Aware Fill and Neural Filters to the forefront, making tasks like object removal, image enhancements, and stylistic adjustments easier than ever.

Content-Aware Fill: Smarter and More Accurate Than Ever

Content-Aware Fill has been a hallmark of Photoshop for years, but with Photoshop 2025, Adobe has expanded its functionality, making it smarter and more accurate than ever. This AI-powered tool automatically removes undesired items or people from an image and intelligently fills in the background with pixels that fit the surrounding surroundings.

How Content-Aware Fill Works in Photoshop 2025:

1. **Select the Unwanted Object**: Use any selection tool (such as the **Lasso Tool**, **Marquee Tool**, or **Quick Selection Tool**) to select the object you want to remove from the image.

2. **Activate Content-Aware Fill**: After making the selection, go to **Edit > Fill** and choose **Content-Aware** from the dropdown menu. Photoshop will automatically analyze the surrounding pixels and fill in the selected area seamlessly.

3. **Refining the Fill**: In Photoshop 2025, the **Content-Aware Fill** workspace has been upgraded to provide more control over how the fill is applied. You can preview the result in real-time and adjust the **sampling area** to fine-tune the fill. Additionally, the **Fill Settings** panel gives you more options for controlling how the fill blends with the surrounding content.

4. **Output to a New Layer**: For greater flexibility, you can output the content-aware fill to a new layer. This allows you to adjust the fill and surrounding areas independently without affecting the original image.

Content-Aware Fill in Photoshop 2025 is extremely powerful when removing larger, more complicated objects or when working with photographs that have detailed backgrounds. The AI advancements make the tool even more efficient, helping you remove items while keeping the overall texture and complexity of the image.

Neural Filters: AI-Driven Image Enhancements

Another outstanding feature of Photoshop 2025 is the introduction of Neural effects, which leverage AI technology to deliver non-destructive, customisable effects that can totally transform a picture. These filters leverage machine learning to assess and apply complicated effects like colorization, style transfer, facial tweaks, and more.

How to Use Neural Filters in Photoshop 2025:

1. **Open the Neural Filters Panel**: To access Neural Filters, go to **Filter > Neural Filters**. This will open the **Neural Filters** workspace, where you can choose from a range of AI-powered effects.

2. **Choose a Filter**: Photoshop 2025 offers several Neural Filters, such as:

   ○ **Skin Smoothing**: AI-powered skin retouching that smooths skin textures while preserving details like pores and natural shadows.

   ○ **Style Transfer**: Apply artistic styles (such as paintings or sketches) to your image based on machine learning models of famous artists.

   ○ **Smart Portrait**: Use this filter to adjust facial features like age, expression, gaze direction, and more, with just a few sliders.

   ○ **Colorize**: Automatically add color to black-and-white photos using AI.

   ○ **Super Zoom**: Enhance image resolution by enlarging your image while maintaining detail, powered by machine learning.

3. **Adjust Settings**: After selecting a filter, you can fine-tune the settings. Each filter offers different sliders or controls that let you refine the effect, such as adjusting the intensity, blending mode, or other parameters.

4. **Preview and Apply**: Use the preview button to see how the filter affects the image in real-time. Once you're happy with the result, click **OK** to apply the filter to your image.

Neural Filters in Photoshop 2025 open up exciting new possibilities for creative professionals. Whether you're retouching portraits, colorizing old photos, or adding artistic flair to your designs, the AI-powered filters make it easier to achieve high-quality results in less time.

Refined Selection Tools: Auto-Select and Select Subject Enhancements

Selection tools are among the most frequently used tools in Photoshop, and with Photoshop 2025, Adobe has updated its selection capabilities to deliver even more precision and efficiency. The inclusion of Auto-Select and upgraded Select Subject features makes it easier to separate complex objects and areas in your photographs with no effort.

Auto-Select: Automatically Selecting Layers with One Click

Auto-Select is a new tool in Photoshop 2025 that simplifies the process of selecting layers in complex documents. This feature automatically chooses the layer beneath the cursor, making it excellent for swiftly picking and working with several levels in a design or composite.

How to Use Auto-Select:

1. **Activate Auto-Select**: In the **Layers Panel**, ensure the **Auto-Select** option is checked. You can choose to auto-select either **Layer** or **Group**.

2. **Click on the Layer**: With **Auto-Select** enabled, simply click on an element in your document, and Photoshop will automatically select the corresponding layer in the **Layers Panel**.

3. **Move and Edit the Layer**: Once selected, you can move, transform, or apply adjustments to the layer. This feature is especially useful for working with complex multi-layer compositions where quickly selecting individual layers can be time-consuming.

Auto-Select streamlines your workflow when working with layered designs or composite images, saving you time and reducing frustration when navigating complex documents.

Enhanced Select Subject: Faster, More Accurate Selections

The **Select Subject** tool is another feature that has seen significant improvements in Photoshop 2025. This AI-powered tool intelligently identifies and selects the main subject in an image, making it easier to isolate objects from complex backgrounds.

How to Use Select Subject in Photoshop 2025:

1. **Activate Select Subject**: Go to **Select > Subject**, and Photoshop will automatically analyze the image to identify the primary subject.

2. **Refine the Selection**: While the selection is usually accurate, you can fine-tune it using the **Select and Mask** workspace or the **Quick Selection Tool** to add or remove areas from the selection.

3. **Use in Compositing**: The refined **Select Subject** feature is perfect for quick masking, background removal, and compositing work. It's especially helpful when isolating objects with intricate edges, such as hair or fur.

With the improved **Select Subject** tool, you can quickly and accurately isolate complex subjects, enabling faster editing, masking, and compositing.

Customizable Workspaces and New UI Changes

Photoshop 2025 features various UI enhancements and expanded customisable workspaces to improve your overall experience. Whether you're working on a small laptop screen or a huge desktop setup, the new interface options and adjustable layouts provide greater flexibility, allowing you to adapt your workspace to meet your needs.

Customizable Workspaces: Tailor Your Environment

In Photoshop 2025, you can now customize your workspace more easily, saving time and improving efficiency by arranging panels, tools, and menus in a way that works best for you.

How to Customize Your Workspace:

1. **Move Panels**: Simply drag panels like **Layers**, **Properties**, and **Histogram** to different positions within the workspace. You can stack them vertically or horizontally or even group them into a floating window.

2. **Create a New Workspace**: Go to **Window > Workspace > New Workspace**, and Photoshop will save your current layout for easy access in the future.

3. **Reset Workspace**: If you ever want to return to the default layout, simply go to **Window > Workspace > Reset [Workspace Name]** to restore the original setup.

The ability to create **custom workspaces** is invaluable for users who work across different types of projects, as it allows you to create a tailored setup for design, photography, or illustration.

New UI Changes: More Intuitive and Accessible

The user interface in Photoshop 2025 has also been updated to improve accessibility and ease of use. Adobe has focused on making the interface more intuitive for both new and experienced users.

Key UI Changes:

1. **Streamlined Toolbars**: Photoshop 2025 has made the **Tools Panel** more streamlined by grouping similar tools together, reducing clutter, and making it easier to access the tools you need.

2. **Improved Dark Mode**: The **Dark Mode** has been enhanced to provide better contrast and legibility, especially for users who spend long hours working in Photoshop.

3. **Touch-Friendly UI**: For users working on touch-enabled devices, Photoshop 2025 introduces a more touch-friendly UI, making it easier to interact with the program using touch gestures.

These **UI updates** and enhancements ensure that Photoshop remains accessible, user-friendly, and efficient, whether you're working on a high-end desktop workstation or a portable device.

Enhanced Performance for Large Files: Improved Speed and Efficiency

Working with enormous files in Photoshop has always been a difficulty, especially when dealing with high-resolution photos, multi-layered compositions, or projects that entail precise details. Photoshop 2025 solves these performance constraints with better speed and efficiency, making it easier to work with huge files without suffering delays or crashes.

Why Performance Matters for Large Files

As the intricacy of a project rises, Photoshop's performance can be significantly hampered. High-resolution photographs, especially ones with numerous layers, demand tremendous memory and computing power. Performance difficulties such as latency, extended rendering periods, or delayed reaction to brush strokes can limit creativity and postpone the execution of assignments.

The introduction of **Photoshop 2025** brings several performance improvements, ensuring that even the largest files can be handled with greater ease.

Key Performance Enhancements in Photoshop 2025

1. **Improved Multi-Core Support**: Photoshop 2025 now utilizes **multi-core processing** more effectively, leveraging the power of modern processors to perform tasks like **filter application**, **image rendering**, and **layer manipulation** much faster. This ensures smoother operation when working with large files or complex compositions, significantly reducing processing times.

2. **Enhanced GPU Acceleration**: Adobe has made improvements to **GPU acceleration**, which is crucial for tasks like applying filters, resizing images, or working with 3D elements. The faster GPU performance enhances your ability to work with high-resolution images or multi-layered files, minimizing lag and speeding up the overall editing process.

3. **Efficient Memory Usage**: Photoshop 2025 has optimized **memory management**, ensuring that Photoshop uses system RAM more efficiently when working with large files. This allows you to open and work with larger images without the risk of running out of memory or slowing down the application.

4. **Faster File Opening and Saving**: The improved file-handling capabilities in Photoshop 2025 mean that even large PSD or TIFF files open and save much faster than in previous versions. This speeds up your overall workflow, reducing downtime when working with heavy files.

5. **Real-Time Performance for Brushes and Tools**: One of the most noticeable improvements is the real-time performance when using **brush tools** or **painting** in Photoshop. You'll experience smoother brush strokes and reduced latency, especially when working with large canvas sizes.

These enhancements make Photoshop 2025 a faster, more efficient tool for professionals working with high-resolution imagery, enabling a more fluid and productive creative process, even with the most demanding files.

New 3D and Video Editing Tools

In addition to improvements in performance, Photoshop 2025 provides new capabilities for 3D and video editing, making it an even more adaptable program for digital artists and designers that work across diverse media.

3D Tools: Enhancing Your Designs with Depth and Dimension

While Photoshop has long supported 3D design, Photoshop 2025 takes 3D creation and manipulation to the next level, giving new tools and features that allow users to build and edit 3D objects, textures, and lighting effects with ease.

Key New 3D Features in Photoshop 2025:

1. **Advanced 3D Textures and Materials**: Photoshop 2025 includes **new, high-quality textures** and **materials** that allow for more realistic 3D designs. These textures are now more customizable and easier to apply, offering a wider range of options for artists who want to add fine details to their 3D models.

2. **Improved 3D Editing and Painting**: The **3D Workspace** has been streamlined, making it easier to create and manipulate 3D objects directly within Photoshop. You can now

paint **textures** directly onto 3D models using brushes, allowing you to add intricate details and realistic surface finishes.

3. **Better Lighting Control**: With improved **lighting controls**, you can create more realistic 3D renders. The new **light options** allow for better shadow creation, adding depth and realism to your 3D projects.

4. **Faster Rendering**: The **rendering process** for 3D models has been optimized, significantly reducing the time it takes to render 3D designs. This allows you to iterate more quickly and achieve the desired results in less time.

Video Editing: Editing and Enhancing Your Video Content in Photoshop

Photoshop 2025 now features more extensive video editing tools, making it easier for users to integrate motion graphics into their workflows. While Photoshop is not a full-fledged video editor, these new video capabilities allow you to make short changes, apply visual effects, and enhance video content without needing to leave the software.

Key New Video Editing Features in Photoshop 2025:

1. **Improved Timeline**: Photoshop 2025 introduces a **more intuitive timeline interface** for video editing. You can now easily trim, cut, and arrange clips, as well as adjust the speed of video elements. This streamlined interface makes working with video content more accessible and less complex.

2. **Enhanced Frame Animation**: Frame-by-frame animation in Photoshop 2025 has been enhanced with better **frame management** and **onion skinning** options, which allow you to visualize and tweak your animations more effectively.

3. **New Video Filters and Effects**: Photoshop 2025 includes several **new video effects** and **filters** that you can apply to video layers. These include **motion blur**, **color correction**, and **lighting effects**, which help to add cinematic polish to your videos.

4. **Audio Editing**: You can now edit and adjust the **audio tracks** of your video content directly within Photoshop. This feature eliminates the need to jump between different software programs when working on video projects, offering a more seamless editing experience.

These new tools open up a whole new world of creative possibilities for those who want to incorporate video into their work or create motion graphics alongside still images.

One of the outstanding aspects of Photoshop 2025 is its expanded connection with Adobe Creative Cloud and third-party programs, allowing users to work effortlessly across numerous platforms and applications. Whether you're working with Adobe Illustrator, After Effects, or third-party design tools, Photoshop's ability to interface with other programs improves your workflow and makes it easier to transfer files and materials across applications.

Seamless Creative Cloud Integration

Photoshop 2025 is more closely integrated with **Adobe Creative Cloud**, allowing for a more connected and cohesive creative process. Here are some of the key integration improvements:

1. **Cloud Document Syncing**: Photoshop 2025 supports **Cloud Documents**, which means you can store your files in the cloud and access them from any device with an internet connection. This allows you to start working on a project on one device and seamlessly continue editing on another.

2. **Creative Cloud Libraries**: You can now access and share **Creative Cloud Libraries** directly from within Photoshop. This allows you to quickly access and apply assets (such as colors, brushes, and styles) from other Creative Cloud applications, streamlining your design process.

3. **Sharing and Collaboration**: With **cloud collaboration tools**, you can easily share your projects with colleagues or clients and receive feedback in real-time. This is a huge advantage for team-based projects, making it easier to collaborate without the need for file sharing or external communication tools.

Third-Party App Integration

Photoshop 2025 also enhances its **integration with third-party apps**, expanding the software's versatility and ensuring compatibility with a wide range of tools and plugins. This is particularly useful for designers and creatives who work with specialized software or need additional functionality beyond what Photoshop offers.

1. **Importing from Other Apps**: Photoshop now makes it easier to import assets from third-party apps, such as **Affinity Designer** or **Sketch**, ensuring a smooth handoff between applications in your creative suite.

2. **Expanded Plugin Support**: Photoshop 2025 supports a wider range of third-party plugins and extensions, which allows users to add custom functionality to Photoshop that is tailored to their specific needs.

By integrating more tightly with **Creative Cloud** and **third-party tools**, Photoshop 2025 enables users to create more efficiently and collaborate seamlessly across a range of software environments.

Project: Applying AI Features to Speed Up Your Workflow

Now that we've explored some of the new features in Photoshop 2025, it's time to apply them in a practical project. In this section, we'll walk through the process of using **AI features** to speed up your workflow, from **AI-powered editing tools** to **automating repetitive tasks**.

Project Overview: Editing a Portrait Using AI Tools

In this project, we'll use the new **AI-powered features** in Photoshop 2025 to quickly edit a portrait photo. The AI tools will help us remove imperfections, enhance the image, and apply creative effects, saving us time and effort compared to manual editing.

Step 1: Retouching with Neural Filters

1. Open the portrait photo in Photoshop 2025.

2. Go to **Filter > Neural Filters** and apply the **Skin Smoothing** filter. This AI-powered tool automatically smooths out the skin while preserving fine details.

3. Use the **Smart Portrait** filter to adjust the subject's expression, making them appear more relaxed or joyful with just a few slider adjustments.

4. Apply the **Colorize** filter if the photo is black-and-white, using AI to automatically add realistic colors to the image.

Step 2: Background Removal with Content-Aware Fill

1. Use the **Quick Selection Tool** to select the background of the image.

2. Go to **Edit > Fill** and choose **Content-Aware Fill**. Photoshop will automatically remove the selected background and fill the area with pixels from the surrounding environment.

3. Refine the fill by adjusting the **sampling area** and previewing the result in real-time.

Step 3: Final Adjustments with AI-Powered Camera Raw Filter

1. Open the **Camera Raw Filter** to make global adjustments to exposure, contrast, and color.

2. Use the **Enhance Details** feature to improve the resolution and clarity of the image, powered by AI.

Step 4: Saving and Exporting

1. Once you're satisfied with the edits, save the image as a **PSD** to preserve the layers.

2. Export the final version as a **JPEG** or **PNG** for sharing or printing.

By applying these **AI features**, we've drastically sped up the editing process, achieving professional-quality results in a fraction of the time.

Photoshop 2025 delivers a series of strong new capabilities that make image editing faster, more efficient, and more creative. From better performance for huge files to the new 3D and video editing tools, the software continues to push the frontiers of what's possible in digital design. The connectivity with Adobe Creative Cloud and third-party programs ensures that Photoshop remains a primary focus for your creative workflow.

By leveraging AI-powered tools like Content-Aware Fill, Neural Filters, and Select Subject, you can automate time-consuming processes and enhance your efficiency, allowing you to focus on the creative parts of your projects.

Chapter 7

Retouching and Restoration - Enhancing Your Images Like a Pro

In the field of picture editing, retouching and restoration are two of the most valuable talents for any photographer, designer, or digital artist. Whether you're dealing with portraits, landscapes, or historical photographs, the ability to enhance and repair images is vital for achieving polished, professional results. Photoshop has long been the industry standard for retouching and restoration, giving a variety of tools designed to help you repair defects, modify tones, and bring photos back to life.

In this chapter, we will study the basic retouching and restoration techniques in Photoshop 2025, from color correction and blemish removal to the more complicated process of restoring ancient pictures. These strategies will help you boost the quality of your images, restore old photographs to their former splendor, and create faultless portraits that fascinate your audience. Whether you're fixing a digital portrait or breathing new life into a damaged vintage photo, using these tools will boost your skills and give you the confidence to take on any retouching project.

Color Correction: Adjusting White Balance and Tone

One of the first steps in retouching any photograph is verifying that the color balance and tone are accurate. Poor color balance can make a shot look strange, while inappropriate tone alterations might leave the image looking flat or lifeless. Photoshop 2025 has extensive capabilities for color correction, letting you rectify these flaws fast and efficiently.

Understanding White Balance

White balance refers to the act of altering the colors in an image to ensure that whites seem white and colors are reproduced appropriately. Incorrect white balance can result in an image that looks too warm (yellowish) or too cool (bluish). For instance, shots taken under incandescent lighting may appear too warm, while photos taken in shadow could have a chilly, blue hue.

How to Adjust White Balance in Photoshop 2025:

1. **Camera Raw Filter**: The **Camera Raw Filter** in Photoshop 2025 provides a powerful interface for color correction, including **white balance** adjustments.

- Open the image in Photoshop and go to **Filter > Camera Raw Filter**.

- In the Camera Raw workspace, look for the **White Balance** panel on the right side. Here, you'll find two options: **Temperature** and **Tint**.

  - **Temperature** adjusts the image's overall warmth. Move the slider to the left for a cooler (bluish) tone or to the right for a warmer (yellowish) tone.

  - **Tint** adjusts the green-magenta shift. Use the slider to correct color casts that appear in the green-to-magenta spectrum.

2. **Eyedropper Tool**: If the image includes a neutral gray or white object, you can use the **Eyedropper Tool** to sample that color, which will automatically adjust the white balance for you.

   - In the **Camera Raw** window, click the **Eyedropper Tool**, then click on a gray or white area of the image. This will set the white balance and remove any color casts.

Tone Adjustments: Correcting Exposure and Contrast

Once the white balance is set, the next step in color correction is adjusting the **tone** of the image—this refers to the **brightness**, **contrast**, and **exposure**. Even images with correct white balance may still appear too dark or too bright, or lack the depth needed for visual impact.

How to Adjust Tone in Photoshop 2025:

1. **Using the Camera Raw Filter**:

   - In the **Basic** panel of the **Camera Raw Filter**, you can adjust exposure, contrast, highlights, shadows, whites, and blacks.

   - **Exposure**: Adjusts the overall brightness of the image.

   - **Contrast**: Increases or decreases the difference between light and dark areas.

   - **Highlights** and **Shadows**: Fine-tune the bright and dark areas separately. For example, use **Shadows** to brighten the darker areas without affecting the highlights.

- ○ **Whites** and **Blacks**: Control the brightest and darkest parts of the image for more control over the tonal range.

2. **Levels and Curves**:

   - ○ For more precise tone adjustments, **Levels** and **Curves** are excellent tools. These allow you to adjust the **tonal range** and **contrast** at a more granular level.

   - ○ Go to **Image > Adjustments > Levels** or **Curves** to access these tools.

     - In the **Levels** window, you'll find sliders for the **Shadows**, **Midtones**, and **Highlights**, which allow you to adjust the image's tonal range.

     - **Curves** give you more control over individual brightness levels, allowing you to adjust the tonal curve to lighten or darken specific areas of the image.

3. **Brightness/Contrast**:

   - ○ You can also use the **Brightness/Contrast** adjustment layer for more straightforward control. This is a simple way to tweak overall exposure and contrast without getting into detailed curves.

By adjusting **white balance** and **tone**, you can ensure that your images have accurate colors and a well-balanced exposure, which is the foundation for creating professional-looking edits.

Removing Blemishes and Imperfections in Portraits

When working with portrait photography, **removing blemishes** and **imperfections** is a crucial part of the retouching process. Whether you're smoothing skin, eliminating acne, or correcting lighting flaws, Photoshop 2025 offers a range of tools designed for portrait retouching.

The Healing Brush and Spot Healing Brush

The **Healing Brush** and **Spot Healing Brush** are two powerful tools for fixing imperfections like pimples, scars, or uneven skin tone.

How to Use the Healing Brush:

1. Select the **Healing Brush Tool** from the **Tools Panel** or press **J**.

2. Hold **Alt** (Windows) or **Option** (Mac) and click to sample an area of clean skin near the blemish.

3. Paint over the imperfection, and Photoshop will blend the surrounding pixels to seamlessly fill in the area.

   o The **Healing Brush Tool** works well for more complex blemishes because it samples from a specific area, ensuring that texture and color match.

How to Use the Spot Healing Brush:

1. Select the **Spot Healing Brush Tool** (also available from the **Tools Panel**).

2. Simply brush over the blemish or imperfection, and Photoshop will automatically fill it in with surrounding textures.

   o The **Spot Healing Brush** is ideal for smaller imperfections and can be used without manually sampling an area.

The Clone Stamp Tool for Precise Removal

The **Clone Stamp Tool** (S) is another essential tool for retouching. While the Healing Brush automatically blends pixels, the **Clone Stamp** duplicates pixels from one part of the image to another, allowing for more controlled and precise fixes.

How to Use the Clone Stamp Tool:

1. Select the **Clone Stamp Tool** from the **Tools Panel** or press **S**.

2. Hold **Alt** (Windows) or **Option** (Mac) and click on an area of skin near the blemish to sample the pixels.

3. Paint over the blemish or imperfection. Adjust the **brush size** and **hardness** in the **Options Bar** for more precision.

Frequency Separation for Skin Smoothing

For more advanced skin retouching, frequency separation allows you to smooth skin while keeping texture. This technique separates the high-frequency (texture) and low-frequency (color and tone) layers of an image, making it easier to repair uneven skin tone and smooth skin without losing detail.

How to Apply Frequency Separation:

1. **Duplicate Layers**: Duplicate your image layer twice. The first duplicate will be used for the **low-frequency** layer (color adjustments), and the second for the **high-frequency** layer (texture).

2. **Apply Gaussian Blur to the Low-Frequency Layer**: On the low-frequency layer, go to **Filter > Blur > Gaussian Blur** and apply a blur to smooth the skin's tone.

3. **Apply High Pass Filter to the High-Frequency Layer**: On the high-frequency layer, use **Filter > Other > High Pass** to preserve the texture while blurring the color.

4. **Use the Healing Brush or Clone Stamp**: After separating the frequencies, use the **Healing Brush** or **Clone Stamp** tool to work on each layer independently, smoothing skin and correcting color inconsistencies.

Frequency separation is a powerful technique that professionals use to create smooth, natural skin textures in portraits while preserving important details like pores and wrinkles.

Restoring Old Photos: Fixing Damage and Enhancing Quality

Restoring antique pictures is one of the most satisfying chores in Photoshop. Whether you're working with historical images, family photos, or vintage prints, Photoshop offers a variety of tools to restore damaged or fading images and bring them back to life.

Repairing Rips, Tears, and Scratches

Many vintage images suffer from physical deterioration such as rips, tears, or scratches. Photoshop's Healing Brush and Clone Stamp are wonderful tools for mending certain types of damage.

How to Repair Damage in Photos:

1. **Select the Healing Brush Tool** and sample an area of clean background near the tear.

2. Paint over the damaged area, allowing Photoshop to blend the pixels seamlessly.

3. For more detailed repairs, use the **Clone Stamp Tool** to duplicate surrounding areas and replace the damaged part.

Restoring Faded Colors and Contrast

Old photos often suffer from **color fading**, leaving them looking washed out. Photoshop 2025 offers tools like **Curves**, **Levels**, and **Hue/Saturation** to restore vibrancy and contrast.

How to Restore Colors:

1. **Use the Curves Adjustment**: Open the **Curves** adjustment layer and adjust the individual RGB channels to restore balance and vibrancy.

2. **Adjust Contrast**: Use the **Levels** adjustment to increase contrast and bring back the detail in shadows and highlights.

3. **Use Hue/Saturation**: To correct specific color imbalances, use the **Hue/Saturation** adjustment to fine-tune colors and restore natural hues.

Fixing Faded or Yellowing Photos

Old photographs, especially those printed on acidic paper, often develop a **yellowish tint** over time. The **Selective Color** tool in Photoshop can help fix this issue by targeting specific color channels.

How to Fix Yellowing:

1. **Open the Selective Color Tool**: Go to **Image > Adjustments > Selective Color**.

2. **Adjust the Yellows**: In the Selective Color menu, adjust the **yellow** slider to reduce the yellowing and restore natural tones.

3. **Fine-Tune with Curves**: For more control over color, use the **Curves** tool to adjust the **blue** and **red** channels for a more neutral look.

Sharpening and Enhancing Image Quality

Once the damage has been repaired and the colors restored, you can use tools like **Sharpen**, **Camera Raw**, and **High Pass Filter** to enhance image quality and improve sharpness.

How to Enhance Image Quality:

1. **Apply the Camera Raw Filter**: Use the **Camera Raw Filter** to sharpen details, reduce noise, and adjust overall exposure.

2. **Use High Pass Filter for Sharpening**: Convert the image to a **Smart Object**, apply a **High Pass Filter**, and set the layer to **Overlay** for sharp, crisp details.

3. **Final Adjustments**: Make any necessary adjustments to contrast, brightness, or saturation to ensure the restored image looks vibrant and detailed.

Hair Retouching Techniques for Natural Results

When it comes to photo retouching, hair is one of the trickiest components to work with. The idea is to improve the hair while retaining its natural texture and flow. Over-processing or making hair appear too flawless can result in an unrealistic effect, but with the appropriate techniques, you can produce realistic and professional results that showcase the subject's hair in the most attractive way possible.

Key Hair Retouching Tools in Photoshop 2025

1. **The Brush Tool**: The **Brush Tool** (B) is essential for painting and enhancing hair texture. Whether you're fixing flyaways or adding volume, a soft, pressure-sensitive brush can help create the illusion of natural, flowing hair.

2. **The Clone Stamp Tool**: The **Clone Stamp Tool** (S) is excellent for fixing small patches of hair or removing stray strands that may be distracting. It works by sampling nearby pixels and painting them over unwanted areas, maintaining the natural look of the hair.

3. **The Healing Brush Tool**: The **Healing Brush Tool** (J) is great for fixing imperfections in hair, such as split ends or stray strands, by blending them seamlessly with the surrounding hair. It's especially useful for smoothing out uneven textures while maintaining the original look.

4. **The Smudge Tool**: The **Smudge Tool** (R) is perfect for **softening** hard edges in the hair and blending in stray strands. This tool is often used to refine the natural flow of hair, especially when you want to smooth out areas that might have been over-sharpened.

How to Retouch Hair in Photoshop 2025:

1. **Fixing Flyaways with the Brush Tool**:

   ○ Select the **Brush Tool** and choose a soft round brush with low opacity.

   ○ Sample the color of the hair from an adjacent area using the **Eyedropper Tool** (I).

   ○ Lightly paint over the flyaways or stray hairs to blend them with the surrounding hair, ensuring a natural flow.

2. **Removing Stray Hairs with the Clone Stamp Tool**:

   ○ Select the **Clone Stamp Tool** and set the brush to a soft, small size.

   ○ Alt-click (Windows) or Option-click (Mac) to sample an area of clean hair.

   ○ Paint over the stray hairs, ensuring you match the direction and texture of the natural hair flow.

3. **Smoothing and Blending with the Healing Brush Tool**:

   ○ Use the **Healing Brush Tool** to gently brush over any small imperfections or uneven textures in the hair.

   ○ Adjust the brush size to fit the area you're working on, and make sure the source point blends seamlessly with the surrounding hair.

4. **Refining the Hair with the Smudge Tool**:

   ○ Select the **Smudge Tool** and set the strength to a low setting (around 10-15%).

   ○ Gently drag along the edges of the hair to soften and refine the flow, creating a more natural look.

Hair retouching in Photoshop requires patience and attention to detail, but with these techniques, you can make subtle improvements that enhance the overall look of your portraits without sacrificing realism.

Removing Backgrounds and Adding New Elements Seamlessly

Removing a backdrop or adding new features to an image is a crucial skill in compositing and retouching. Whether you're isolating a subject for a new surroundings, replacing a drab background, or integrating numerous photographs into one, Photoshop offers a suite of tools that make these operations easier and more exact.

The Quick Selection Tool and Select Subject

The Quick Selection Tool (W) and Select Subject function in Photoshop 2025 make it exceedingly easy to isolate subjects from their surroundings. The Select topic function employs AI-driven technology to accurately recognize and select the main topic in your image, while the Quick Selection Tool allows you to refine the selection manually.

How to Remove a Background Using Select Subject:

1. **Select the Subject**: Go to **Select > Subject**, and Photoshop will automatically select the main subject in the image.

2. **Refine the Selection**: Use the **Quick Selection Tool** to add or remove areas from the selection. Hold the **Alt/Option** key to subtract, or simply brush over the areas you want to add to the selection.

3. **Create a Layer Mask**: Once the subject is selected, add a **Layer Mask** to hide the background. You can further refine the mask using the **Select and Mask** workspace for more detailed adjustments.

4. **Add a New Background**: After removing the old background, you can easily add a new background layer. Import the new background image and position it beneath the subject layer. Use **Blend Modes** and **Layer Adjustments** to match the lighting and tone of the new background to the subject.

Using the Pen Tool for Precision Selections

For more complex images with intricate edges, such as hair or fur, the **Pen Tool** (P) is an excellent choice for making precise selections. While the **Quick Selection Tool** can handle most tasks, the **Pen Tool** allows you to create paths that give you full control over the selection.

How to Use the Pen Tool for Background Removal:

1. **Create a Path**: Select the **Pen Tool** and begin clicking around the subject to create anchor points. Make sure to follow the contour of the subject closely for an accurate path.

2. **Convert the Path to a Selection**: After completing the path, right-click and choose **Make Selection**. Adjust the feathering if necessary to soften the edges.

3. **Refine and Mask**: Once the selection is created, apply a **Layer Mask** to hide the background. You can refine the mask using the **Brush Tool** to clean up any rough edges.

These techniques allow for fast and precise removal of backgrounds, enabling you to seamlessly integrate subjects into new environments or composite images.

Working with Textures: Using Overlay and Pattern Layers

Textures serve a significant part in providing realism and visual interest to an image. Whether you're working with textures for backdrops, apparel, or artistic effects, Photoshop 2025 provides powerful capabilities to apply and modify textures seamlessly using overlay layers and pattern layers.

Using Overlay Layers for Textures

An Overlay layer is a common approach to apply textures to an image while allowing the underlying colors and features to shine through. The Overlay Blending Mode is used to merge the texture with the image in a way that highlights the details without overpowering the composition.

How to Use Overlay Layers for Textures:

1. **Select Your Texture**: Open the texture file in Photoshop. You can use textures such as paper, fabric, grunge, or natural textures like wood or stone.

2. **Place the Texture Layer**: Drag the texture into your main image and position it on a new layer.

3. **Set the Blending Mode to Overlay**: In the **Layers Panel**, change the **Blending Mode** of the texture layer to **Overlay**. This will blend the texture with the image while maintaining the brightness and contrast of the underlying colors.

4. **Adjust Opacity**: You can reduce the **opacity** of the texture layer to control the intensity of the effect, ensuring that the texture doesn't overpower the subject.

Overlay layers are ideal for adding realistic details to an image, such as simulating light reflections, textures on surfaces, or subtle artistic effects.

Using Pattern Layers for Seamless Textures

Pattern layers are useful when you need to create repeating textures or fill large areas with consistent patterns. Photoshop allows you to create custom patterns and apply them to your image for added depth and interest.

How to Use Pattern Layers:

1. **Create or Import a Pattern**: Go to **Edit > Define Pattern** to create a custom pattern from any image or texture. Alternatively, you can use Photoshop's built-in patterns.

2. **Apply the Pattern**: Select the **Pattern Stamp Tool** or create a new **Fill Layer** and choose **Pattern** from the **Fill Options**.

3. **Adjust the Scale**: Use the **Pattern Fill** settings to adjust the scale and orientation of the pattern to fit your design.

4. **Masking**: Apply a **Layer Mask** to blend the pattern seamlessly into your composition. You can also use a **Gaussian Blur** to soften the pattern for a more natural look.

Pattern layers are particularly useful for creating backgrounds or surface details that require repetition, such as fabric textures or tiled designs.

Project: Restoring and Enhancing a Vintage Photograph

In this project, we will apply the techniques learned in this chapter to **restore and enhance a vintage photograph**. This process involves removing imperfections, fixing damaged areas, enhancing the image quality, and adding creative textures to bring the photo back to life.

Step 1: Assessing the Image

Start by assessing the damage in the vintage photo. Common issues with old photographs include **fading, scratches, tears**, and **color discoloration**. Take note of the areas that require the most attention, such as the background, subject, and edges.

Step 2: Repairing Scratches and Blemishes

1. **Use the Healing Brush Tool** to fix small scratches and blemishes on the photo.

2. **Clone Stamp Tool**: For larger or more complex damage, use the **Clone Stamp Tool** to sample nearby areas and cover the damaged sections.

Step 3: Enhancing Colors and Tone

1. **Color Correction**: Use the **Camera Raw Filter** to adjust the exposure, contrast, and white balance, restoring the colors to their original vibrancy.

2. **Apply Curves**: Adjust the overall tonal range of the photo to increase contrast and restore lost details in the highlights and shadows.

Step 4: Adding Texture

1. **Overlay Layer**: Apply a subtle **grunge texture** using an **Overlay** layer to add depth and realism to the restored photo.

2. **Pattern Layer**: If you want to add texture to the background, use a **pattern layer** to create a seamless effect.

Step 5: Final Touches and Exporting

Once you've restored and enhanced the image, perform any final touch-ups, such as adding more contrast or smoothing out areas. When satisfied with the result, save the restored photo as a **PSD** file for further editing, and export the final version as a **JPEG** or **PNG** for printing or sharing.

Retouching and restoring photographs is an essential skill for any digital artist or photographer, and Photoshop 2025 gives a strong range of tools to accomplish immaculate results. From hair retouching and blemish removal to backdrop replacement and restoring vintage photos, Photoshop gives you the power to bring your images to life with precision and ease.

In this chapter, we've explored basic techniques for retouching portraits, removing backgrounds, dealing with textures, and repairing ancient pictures. These skills are necessary for attaining excellent outcomes in digital image enhancement and restoration. With these techniques, you can take any image—whether it's a modern portrait or a damaged old photo—and improve it to perfection.

Chapter 8

Creative Compositing – Combining Multiple Images for Stunning Results

---

Compositing is one of the most fun and powerful parts of picture alteration in Photoshop. It allows you to integrate many photos into a single, cohesive piece of art, generating visually fascinating and unusual creations. Whether you're combining aspects of a landscape, integrating pictures with creative backgrounds, or making sophisticated digital artwork, compositing in Photoshop provides you the versatility to craft whatever you desire.

Creative compositing includes more than just layering photos together; it's about smoothly integrating those images so that they look like they were always meant to be part of the same scene. In Photoshop, layer masks, blending modes, and numerous editing tools provide you the accuracy needed to bring together disparate visual aspects.

In this chapter, we will study how to mix various photos to create magnificent compositions. We'll go into the essential concepts of layer masking for non-destructive compositing, blending numerous photos together using lighting, shadows, and color matching, and how to make your composites look polished, realistic, and professional.

By the end of this chapter, you will understand how to edit and integrate distinct visual elements, adding depth, contrast, and creativity to your composite designs. Whether you're making a movie poster, creating conceptual artwork, or just experimenting with your picture, understanding compositing in Photoshop will substantially boost your editing skills.

Compositing: Combining Images Seamlessly

Compositing, in its core, is the art of blending numerous distinct images into one seamless final product. While it might sound straightforward, the trick to making high-quality composites rests in learning how to match lighting, shadows, and color between the many photos. In Photoshop, these tactics are made easier with layer-based processes, allowing you to control each piece independently without influencing others.

Understanding the Basics of Compositing in Photoshop

Compositing begins by picking the photos you want to mix. These photos could come from different sources, and it's crucial to guarantee that they can function together cohesively. A effective composite requires you to focus on a few important elements:

1. **Matching Light and Shadows**: When you combine multiple images, it's essential to ensure that the lighting in each image matches. Different light sources and angles can create an unrealistic look if not corrected.

2. **Blending Edges and Transitions**: Sharp edges from one image may look unnatural when placed against another. Proper blending of edges is crucial to creating a seamless transition between the different parts of the composite.

3. **Color Matching**: Colors from each image must blend naturally. The color palette should be consistent across the composite to make it feel unified.

Steps to Start a Basic Composite:

1. **Select Your Images**: Choose the images you want to combine. For example, you may want to use a model photo and place them against a new background.

2. **Open in Photoshop**: Open all images as separate layers within one Photoshop document. You can also **drag and drop** images directly into your working file.

3. **Arrange the Images**: Position each image in its own layer. Ensure that each layer is aligned correctly. The model image might be placed on top, while the background is placed below.

The power of compositing lies in your ability to make these separate images work together harmoniously. For this, understanding how to use **layer masks** and **adjustments** is key.

Using Layer Masks for Non-Destructive Compositing

One of the most effective tools in Photoshop for compositing is the Layer Mask. Layer masks are non-destructive tools that allow you to hide areas of a layer, revealing what is beneath it. This is vital when integrating numerous photographs, as you might need to hide elements of one image to make it fit seamlessly into the composition.

How to Use Layer Masks:

1. **Add a Layer Mask**:

   o Select the layer you want to mask.

   o Click the **Add Layer Mask** icon at the bottom of the **Layers Panel** (it looks like a rectangle with a circle inside).

   o A white thumbnail will appear next to your layer, which represents the visible parts of the layer.

2. **Hide Parts of the Layer**:

   o With the **Layer Mask** selected, use the **Brush Tool** (B) with **black** as your foreground color to paint over the areas you want to hide.

   o Painting with **black** on the mask hides the content of the layer, while painting with **white** restores it. **Gray** tones will partially hide the content, creating soft transitions.

3. **Refining the Mask**:

   o **Feathering**: To create softer transitions, you can **feather** the mask by selecting the mask thumbnail, going to the **Properties Panel**, and adjusting the **Feather** slider. This helps create a smooth, gradual blend between the images.

   o **Refine Mask Edges**: For more complex edges (such as hair), use the **Select and Mask** workspace to refine the mask further.

Benefits of Non-Destructive Editing with Layer Masks:

- **Flexibility**: You can adjust the mask at any time, making it easy to fine-tune your composite.

- **Preserving Image Data**: Layer masks allow you to hide parts of an image without permanently deleting any data, making it easy to recover the original image if necessary.

- **Precision**: By masking out unwanted areas and blending them with other parts of the image, you can create a perfect transition between the elements in the composite.

Practical Use Case: Masking the Model onto the Background

- Open your background image and the model image in Photoshop.

- Place the model image on top of the background layer.

- Add a **Layer Mask** to the model layer and use the **Brush Tool** to paint over the areas you don't want to show, like the edges around the model. This will seamlessly remove the background around the model.

- Refine the mask using **Select and Mask** to make the edges of the model's hair and clothing blend naturally with the background.

Layer masks are essential for achieving a seamless, professional composite by ensuring the images fit together smoothly without destructive edits.

Blending Multiple Images: Lighting, Shadows, and Color Matching

One of the most crucial components of compositing is making sure the photos mix properly, especially in terms of lighting, shadows, and color matching. If these aspects are misaligned, the finished image will look disconnected and unnatural. To produce a coherent composition, you must ensure that lighting conditions and colors match throughout all photographs.

Matching Lighting:

Matching the lighting between distinct photographs can be a tough task, especially if the images were taken in different places with different light sources. However, Photoshop has features to help synchronize the illumination.

Using Adjustment Layers:

1. **Levels and Curves**: Adjustment layers like **Levels** and **Curves** allow you to adjust the brightness, contrast, and tones of each image. These layers can be clipped to specific layers, ensuring that the adjustments only affect the selected layer.

   - **Levels**: Use **Levels** to adjust the overall brightness and contrast of the image. Adjust the **white, black**, and **gray** sliders to match the lighting of the background and foreground elements.

- **Curves**: Use **Curves** for more detailed control over the highlights, shadows, and midtones. You can adjust the red, green, and blue channels to match the color tones of the images.

2. **Using Gradient Map**: The **Gradient Map** adjustment layer is useful for adjusting the color tone of an image. Apply a gradient that matches the overall color temperature of your scene (warm or cool) to blend elements more naturally.

Matching Shadows:

Shadows are crucial to making a composite look realistic, as they help to ground the subject in its new environment. In Photoshop 2025, **casting shadows** in your compositions has become easier with improved tools and brushes.

How to Create Realistic Shadows:

1. **Create a Shadow Layer**: Create a new **Layer** beneath the subject you're working with. Use the **Brush Tool** (B) with a soft round brush and paint black to create a shadow that matches the light direction in your scene.

2. **Adjust the Opacity and Blur**: Lower the opacity of the shadow layer and use **Gaussian Blur** to soften the edges of the shadow. This will give the shadow a more realistic, diffused appearance.

3. **Position and Transform**: Use **Free Transform** (Ctrl+T / Cmd+T) to adjust the shadow's size, rotation, and position so that it aligns with the light source in the image.

Color Matching:

After adjusting the lighting and shadows, the next step is to ensure that the **colors** from all the images in your composite match. Photoshop offers several tools to help you balance the colors and make the images appear as if they were taken under the same conditions.

How to Match Colors:

1. **Match Color Command**: The **Match Color** command (found under **Image > Adjustments > Match Color**) is a quick way to match the color palette of one image to another.

   - Select the **source** (the image you want to match) and adjust the **Luminance** and **Color Intensity** sliders until you achieve a seamless blend.

2. **Selective Color Adjustment**: For more control over the color matching process, use the **Selective Color** adjustment layer. This allows you to adjust specific colors (reds, blues, greens, etc.) to match the tone of the other images in your composition.

Practical Use Case: Blending Multiple Elements

In a typical composite, you might have a model placed in a new environment. To make this work seamlessly, adjust the lighting of the model to match the background:

- **Match the Shadows**: Use the **Brush Tool** to add shadows beneath the model to make them look grounded in the environment.

- **Adjust Color**: Use **Match Color** or **Selective Color** to ensure the model's colors align with the background elements.

Project: Restoring and Enhancing a Vintage Photograph

Now that we've covered the essential compositing techniques, let's apply what we've learned in a practical project. In this project, we'll be restoring and enhancing a **vintage photograph** by adding new elements, correcting colors, and blending everything together seamlessly.

Step 1: Preparing the Vintage Photograph

1. **Open the Image**: Open the vintage photograph in Photoshop. Take note of any damage or fading that may need to be fixed.

2. **Analyze the Lighting**: Study the lighting in the photo. Are there any areas that are too dark or light? If so, use **Curves** or **Levels** to correct these issues.

3. **Repair Damage**: Use the **Healing Brush Tool** or **Clone Stamp Tool** to repair scratches, rips, or stains.

Step 2: Adding New Elements

1. **Import New Elements**: Add new elements, such as a different background or objects, to the composition.

2. **Use Layer Masks**: Apply **Layer Masks** to seamlessly blend the new elements with the original photo, adjusting their position and size to fit the scene.

Step 3: Adjusting Color and Lighting

1. **Adjust Colors**: Use **Match Color** or **Selective Color** to ensure the added elements match the tones of the original photo.

2. **Create Shadows**: Add shadows under new objects or people to ground them in the scene.

3. **Fine-Tune Lighting**: Make adjustments to the overall lighting using **Curves** or **Levels** to ensure the image looks cohesive.

Step 4: Final Refinements and Exporting

1. **Smooth Transitions**: Use **Gaussian Blur** or **Feathering** on the edges of masks to smooth out any hard lines and create seamless transitions.

2. **Save and Export**: Once satisfied with the final result, save your project as a **PSD** file to retain all layers. Export the final image as a **JPEG** or **PNG** for sharing or printing.

Creating Double Exposures and Surreal Effects

One of the most popular and visually impressive compositing techniques is double exposure. This method mixes two or more photos in such a way that their details overlap, generating a dreamy or surreal look. Double exposures are often employed in photography, advertising, and artistic ventures, when the combination of photos delivers a deeper message or tells a story that one image alone cannot.

In Photoshop 2025, achieving multiple exposures and surreal effects has gotten easier because of better blending modes, layer masks, and adjustment layers.

Understanding Double Exposure

Double exposure in digital art frequently entails overlaying one image on top of another, with the purpose of creating a new image where components from both photos seamlessly flow into each other. The secret is in how the images interact—what sections remain visible and what parts get masked or buried.

How to Create Double Exposure in Photoshop 2025:

1. **Choose Your Images**: Start with selecting the two images you want to combine. Typically, one image will be of a subject (like a portrait), and the second image will be

something abstract or environmental (such as nature, architecture, or texture). The images should complement each other in both tone and composition.

2. **Layer the Images**:

   o Open both images in Photoshop.

   o Place the subject image (for example, the portrait) as the base layer.

   o Place the secondary image (for example, a landscape or cityscape) as the top layer.

3. **Apply a Layer Mask**: Add a **Layer Mask** to the top image to control which parts of the image are visible. With the mask selected, use the **Brush Tool** to paint with black over areas that you want to hide, revealing the subject image beneath. Use soft, low-opacity brushes to create smooth transitions between the two images.

4. **Adjust the Blending Mode**:

   o Select the top image layer and experiment with different **blending modes** in the Layers Panel. Blending modes like **Screen** or **Overlay** can be used to combine the images in a way that creates ethereal effects, especially when working with lighter tones.

   o Adjust the opacity of the top layer to control the intensity of the effect.

5. **Fine-Tune with Adjustment Layers**: Use **Adjustment Layers** to match the color tones of the two images. Common adjustments include **Levels, Curves**, and **Hue/Saturation** to fine-tune the contrast, brightness, and color balance between the images.

6. **Refine the Mask**: To achieve a smoother blend, you can refine the **Layer Mask** using the **Select and Mask** workspace. This allows you to soften edges and make the transition between the subject and the background more seamless.

7. **Final Adjustments**: After blending the images, you may want to add additional elements like **light effects** or **grain** to create a more unified look. Layering textures can also add depth and interest to the final image.

Using Surreal Effects to Enhance Your Compositing

Double exposure itself is a surreal effect, but you can take it even further with techniques like **texture overlays**, **color grading**, and **distortions**.

- **Textures**: Adding textures such as **grunge**, **clouds**, or **light leaks** can introduce an additional layer of creativity to your composite, enhancing the surreal or abstract nature of the image.

- **Color Grading**: Adjust the **color tones** to create a dreamlike atmosphere. You can use **Gradient Maps** or **Color Lookup Tables (LUTs)** to give your composite an artistic color palette, enhancing its mood.

- **Distortions and Warps**: The **Liquify Tool** (Filter > Liquify) or the **Puppet Warp** tool can add subtle distortions or surreal bends to objects, faces, or elements within the composite to make them appear more otherworldly.

These techniques can push your composite from a simple combination of two images to something truly unique and imaginative.

Integrating 3D Objects and Textures into Composites

Incorporating 3D objects and textures into your compositing work can take your designs to the next level. Photoshop 2025 makes it easy to combine 3D models, textures, and even textural effects into your 2D creations. Whether you're adding a 3D logo to a photo, integrating 3D elements into a landscape, or creating an entirely new scene with 3D objects, Photoshop's 3D workspace gives you powerful tools to manage and render 3D materials.

Using 3D Objects in Photoshop 2025

Photoshop 2025 has increased its capacity to import and work with 3D objects. You may now incorporate 3D models straight into your project and alter them using 3D tools within Photoshop. Here's how to integrate a 3D item into your composite:

1. **Import a 3D Object**:

   - Go to **3D > New 3D Layer from File** and import a 3D model (in formats like .OBJ or .FBX).

- You can also create a basic 3D object in Photoshop using shapes like cubes or spheres.

2. **Position the 3D Object**:

   - Use the **3D Panel** to manipulate the object's position, scale, and rotation. You can move, scale, and rotate the object in 3D space to fit your composition.

   - Adjust the **perspective** so that the object matches the background in terms of angle and depth.

3. **Apply Materials and Textures**:

   - Apply textures and materials to your 3D objects to match the rest of the composition. Photoshop allows you to drag and drop textures onto 3D surfaces.

   - Use **Material Editor** in the **3D Panel** to tweak properties like **reflectivity**, **glossiness**, and **transparency**.

4. **Lighting and Shadows**:

   - Set up **light sources** within the 3D workspace to cast shadows and highlight certain areas of the 3D object.

   - Adjust the **shadow** and **reflection** settings to make the 3D object blend naturally with the scene.

5. **Rendering the Final Composite**:

   - Once the 3D object is positioned and textured, you can render it to match the lighting and colors of the 2D background.

   - Go to **3D > Render** to complete the process.

This ability to integrate **3D elements** with 2D backgrounds is especially powerful for projects that require high-level **visual effects** or intricate **compositing work**.

Project: Creating a Surreal Landscape Composite

In this project, we'll apply the techniques discussed earlier to create a **surreal landscape composite**. This composite will feature a combination of **realistic landscape images, 3D objects**, and **double exposure effects**.

Step 1: Prepare the Background Image

1. **Select a Landscape Photo**: Start by choosing a dramatic or moody landscape photo—something that has good depth and lighting. A mountainous or forest scene works well for surreal effects.

2. **Adjust the Colors**: Use **Curves** or **Color Lookup** to adjust the tones and give the image an otherworldly feel. Apply a cool, blue-toned color scheme to make the scene feel dreamlike and mysterious.

Step 2: Add the Main Subject (e.g., a Person or Object)

1. **Choose a Subject**: Select an image of a person or object that you want to place into the landscape. This could be a silhouette or something with striking features.

2. **Apply a Layer Mask**: Use a **Layer Mask** to carefully remove the background from the subject. Use the **Pen Tool** or **Quick Selection Tool** for precision. Once the subject is isolated, place them onto the landscape layer.

3. **Blend the Subject**: Apply **color grading** to match the subject's tones with the environment. Adjust the **shadows** and **highlights** to blend them smoothly into the new setting.

Step 3: Add Surreal Elements (e.g., Floating Objects)

1. **Import 3D Objects or Textures**: Add surreal objects, such as floating orbs, geometric shapes, or abstract structures. Import 3D objects and use **layer masks** and **adjustment layers** to blend them naturally into the scene.

2. **Apply Lighting**: Add a soft glow or ethereal lighting to the floating objects. Use the **Glow** effect or create custom lighting with the **Brush Tool** to enhance the surreal atmosphere.

Step 4: Integrate Double Exposure Effect

1. **Double Exposure**: Choose an image (such as a tree or stars) and apply the **double exposure** technique to blend it with the subject. Use **layer masks** to reveal portions of the second image and adjust the **opacity** and **blending modes** to achieve the right effect.

2. **Refine Transitions**: Use the **Smudge Tool** or **Brush Tool** to soften any harsh lines and create smooth transitions between the subject and the double exposure elements.

Step 5: Final Adjustments

1. **Enhance with Shadows and Highlights**: Add **shadows** where necessary to ground the floating objects and integrate them seamlessly. Use the **Dodge and Burn** tools to enhance the lighting and create more contrast.

2. **Apply Final Color Grading**: Use **Gradient Maps**, **Selective Color** adjustments, and **Hue/Saturation** to perfect the overall color palette and unify the composition.

3. **Sharpen the Image**: Apply **sharpening** to enhance the details, especially around the subject and 3D objects, using the **High Pass Filter** method.

In this chapter, we've studied the power and adaptability of creative compositing in Photoshop 2025. From creating double exposures and surreal effects to integrating 3D objects and textures, these techniques allow you to integrate many photos smoothly and create striking, innovative compositions. Through the step-by-step project, you've learned how to merge fact with imagination to produce a surreal landscape composite that appears both professional and captivating.

Mastering compositing in Photoshop brings up unlimited opportunities for digital artists, designers, and photographers. Whether you're working on conceptual art, advertising ideas, or creative photography, the tools and approaches presented in this chapter will help you generate visually beautiful outcomes.

Chapter 9

Working with Video and Animation – Motion Graphics in Photoshop

When you think of Adobe Photoshop, the first thing that usually springs to mind is photo editing. However, with each succeeding iteration, Photoshop has evolved into a flexible multimedia application. While still the go-to application for image alteration, Photoshop has rapidly become a helpful resource for dealing with video and animation as well. Photoshop 2025 follows this trend, giving extensive tools for video editing, motion graphics, and rudimentary animation, making it a great alternative for producers who seek to merge still photography with motion.

Surprisingly, Photoshop's video editing capabilities are often underestimated. Yet, Photoshop offers remarkable features for manipulating video footage, producing cinematic effects, and designing motion graphics. These capabilities allow users to mix spectacular images with the seamless integration of video, and they do so in a way that stays accessible to both beginners and seasoned makers alike.

In this chapter, we will introduce you to Photoshop's video editing skills, including how to build up a basic video timeline, how to import and edit clips, and how to utilize layers and keyframes to create simple animations. Whether you're a photographer who wants to dip your toes into video editing, a designer adding animations to your projects, or a creative professional exploring the field of motion graphics, learning video editing in Photoshop opens up a new world of possibilities for your work.

Photoshop's Video Editing Capabilities

Photoshop 2025 provides various new capabilities that make video editing and animation easier than ever. While Photoshop has always let users work with video layers, the 2025 version has even more sophisticated capabilities for animating layers, generating motion graphics, and making high-quality video footage. These characteristics make Photoshop a superb alternative for consumers who desire a single software solution for both still image editing and video production.

What Photoshop Offers for Video Editing

1. **Video Layers**: Photoshop allows you to treat video clips as **layers** in the same way you work with images. This gives you the ability to apply **adjustment layers**, **filters**, and **layer styles** to individual video clips, providing a high level of flexibility and creative control.

2. **Timeline Panel**: The **Timeline** is where all the magic happens in Photoshop's video editing workflow. It's a visual representation of your video and animations, showing the timing of your video clips, transitions, and keyframes. In Photoshop 2025, the **Timeline** panel has been enhanced to give you better control over editing and animation.

3. **Non-Destructive Editing**: With **adjustment layers**, **layer masks**, and **smart objects**, Photoshop allows you to make **non-destructive edits** to your video files. This means you can always go back and tweak your edits without permanently altering your original video clip.

4. **Motion Graphics**: One of the standout features of Photoshop for video work is its ability to integrate with **motion graphics**. You can create animated graphics, text effects, and visual elements that can be exported as video files, making it a great tool for creating **advertisements**, **explainer videos**, or even **social media content**.

5. **Keyframe Animation**: Photoshop 2025 adds even more flexibility to animation by allowing you to **animate layers** using **keyframes**. This feature enables you to create movement, transitions, and effects for your video projects, all within Photoshop's intuitive interface.

While Photoshop is not as powerful as dedicated video editing software like Adobe Premiere Pro, it is more than capable of handling **basic video editing tasks** and creating **motion graphics**. With Photoshop's video and animation capabilities, you can edit video files, create layered compositions, and add dynamic effects with ease.

Basic Video Timeline Setup: Importing and Editing Clips

Setting up your video editing workspace in Photoshop begins with the Timeline panel. The Timeline is where you manage and modify all video layers, clip transitions, keyframes, and animations. To get started with video editing, it's vital to learn how to set up your timeline, import your video clips, and grasp how to edit them.

How to Set Up the Video Timeline in Photoshop 2025

1. **Open the Timeline Panel**:

   ○ To start working with video in Photoshop, go to **Window > Timeline** to open the Timeline panel. If you don't see the Timeline option, you might need to switch to the **Motion** workspace.

2. **Create a New Video Project**:

   ○ If you're starting from scratch, go to **File > New** and create a document with your desired dimensions and resolution. Make sure to set the **Background Contents** to transparent and the **Resolution** to 72 pixels/inch if you're working with standard video formats.

   ○ Photoshop will automatically create a blank timeline for you to begin importing and editing video clips.

3. **Import Video Clips**:

   ○ To import video clips into Photoshop, go to **File > Import > Video Frames to Layers**. This will import your video into the Timeline, where each frame will be treated as a layer.

   ○ Alternatively, you can **drag and drop** video files directly into the **Layers Panel**, and Photoshop will automatically create video layers for each clip.

4. **Understanding the Timeline Layout**:

   ○ Once your video clips are imported, the **Timeline** panel will display your video as layers. You'll see each layer in the timeline as a **strip**, showing the duration of the video and individual frames.

   ○ You can control the **in-point** (where the video starts) and **out-point** (where the video ends) by dragging the ends of the video layer in the timeline.

Editing Video Clips on the Timeline

1. **Trim Video Clips**:

   - Use the **Playhead** to scrub through your video clips. To trim a video clip, hover over the beginning or end of the clip in the Timeline and drag to adjust its length.

2. **Move and Arrange Clips**:

   - You can rearrange the order of your video clips by clicking and dragging them in the **Timeline**. This allows you to sequence your clips and create a coherent flow for your video project.

3. **Split and Cut Video Clips**:

   - To cut a video clip into sections, move the **Playhead** to the desired cutting point and press **Ctrl + Shift + K** (Windows) or **Cmd + Shift + K** (Mac). This will **split** the video clip at that point, creating two separate video layers.

4. **Adjust Clip Speed**:

   - You can speed up or slow down a video clip by **right-clicking** on the clip in the Timeline and selecting **Speed/Duration**. Here, you can set the clip's playback speed or apply a time-remapping effect.

Using Layers and Keyframes for Basic Animation

Once you have set up your video clips, the following step is to animate them using layers and keyframes. Keyframe animation allows you to create smooth transitions, movement, and effects by specifying the start and finish locations of an animation. Photoshop's Keyframe capability makes it easy to animate text, graphics, and video clips within the Timeline.

Understanding Keyframes in Photoshop 2025

Keyframes are marks that determine the beginning and ending points of an animation. In Photoshop's video timeline, keyframes are used to manage changes in characteristics like position, opacity, scale, rotation, and effects over time. When you add a keyframe, Photoshop will automatically interpolate the values between the two keyframes, providing a smooth transition.

How to Use Keyframes for Basic Animation:

1. **Enable Keyframe Animation**:

   o To animate a property, click the **Transform** or **Video Layer** dropdown arrow in the **Timeline panel**. You'll see various properties that can be animated, such as **Position**, **Opacity**, **Scale**, **Rotation**, and **Effect**.

   o Click the **clock icon** next to the property you want to animate to add your first keyframe.

2. **Set the First Keyframe**:

   o Move the **Playhead** to the point in time where you want the animation to begin. Set the initial value of the property (e.g., the starting **position** or **opacity**).

   o Once the property is set, click the **Add Keyframe** button (it looks like a diamond) to lock in the value at this specific point in time.

3. **Set the Second Keyframe**:

   o Move the **Playhead** to a new position on the timeline (this is the point where the animation will end).

   o Adjust the property (e.g., change the **position** or **opacity**) to the desired final value.

   o Photoshop will automatically create the second keyframe and interpolate the changes between the two keyframes.

4. **Refining the Animation**:

   o You can create smooth animations by adjusting the **timing** between keyframes. Move the **keyframes** along the timeline to control how fast or slow the transition occurs.

   o To ease the animation and make it more natural, right-click on the keyframes and choose **Ease In** or **Ease Out** to give the animation a more fluid start or end.

5. **Animate Other Properties**:

   ○ Beyond position and opacity, you can also animate **filters** like **blur** or **color effects**. Simply enable keyframes for the desired property and adjust the settings over time.

Animating Text and Motion Graphics:

1. **Animating Text Layers**:

   ○ To animate text, first create a **Text Layer** and enter your desired text. To animate this text, apply keyframes to properties like **position**, **opacity**, and **scale**.

   ○ You can also apply Photoshop's **Text Effects** and animate them using keyframes to create dynamic text animations.

2. **Using Smart Objects**:

   ○ Convert layers into **Smart Objects** to maintain non-destructive editing. This is especially useful for text and other graphical elements that you want to animate repeatedly without losing quality.

Project: Creating a Surreal Landscape Composite with Animation

In this project, we will bring everything we've learned together by creating a **surreal landscape composite** with basic animation. We'll animate elements within the scene, such as floating objects, and use motion graphics to enhance the surreal atmosphere.

Step 1: Set Up the Landscape Background

1. **Import the Landscape**: Start by importing a high-quality landscape image (such as a mountain range or a forest). Adjust the colors and lighting using **Adjustment Layers** to create a more dramatic and surreal tone.

Step 2: Add Floating Objects (e.g., Planets, Stars)

1. **Import 3D Objects**: Use the **3D workspace** to import a 3D model of a planet or other surreal object. Position the object within the scene and adjust its size, rotation, and lighting to fit the atmosphere of the landscape.

2. **Animate the Floating Objects**:

   ○ Use **keyframes** to animate the floating objects, making them slowly drift across the scene. Adjust the **position** and **opacity** over time to create a smooth, ethereal effect.

Step 3: Create Text and Motion Graphics

1. **Add Animated Text**: Add a title or message to the scene using the **Text Tool**. Animate the text by applying **keyframes** to the **position, opacity**, and **scale** properties.

2. **Add Motion Effects**: Use **motion blur** and other filters to add dynamic effects to the text and objects, enhancing the surreal feel of the composition.

Step 4: Final Adjustments and Exporting

1. **Refine the Animation**: Adjust the **timing** of keyframes and smooth transitions between movements. Use **ease in** and **ease out** options to make the animation feel more natural.

2. **Export the Animation**: Once you're satisfied with the animation, export your project as a **GIF, MP4**, or **AVI** file, depending on your desired output format.

Adding Motion to Text, Shapes, and Images

One of the most intriguing aspects of Photoshop 2025 is the ability to apply motion to text, objects, and images to create compelling and dynamic video material. This functionality enables you to make still photos come to life and tells a story through animation.

Whether you're creating animated titles, having graphic components move around the screen, or adding dynamic effects to your photographs, Photoshop allows you the versatility to incorporate movement smoothly.

Adding Motion to Text Text animation is a vital part of motion graphics. In Photoshop, you can animate text to move, fade, scale, or change color over time. This approach is extensively employed in video production, particularly for title sequences, bottom thirds, and end credits.

How to Animate Text in Photoshop 2025:

1. **Create Your Text Layer**:

   - Select the **Text Tool (T)** from the Tools Panel and click on the canvas to create your text. Type in the desired text.

   - Once the text is typed, select the **Move Tool** (V) to position it where you want it to appear in the frame.

2. **Convert to Video Layer**:

   - In the **Timeline Panel**, click on the dropdown next to the text layer, and click **Convert to Video Layer**. This will allow you to animate the text in the timeline.

3. **Add Keyframes**:

   - Move the **Playhead** to the position in the timeline where you want the animation to start.

   - Click the **Transform** icon in the **Timeline** panel and add a **keyframe** by clicking the stopwatch icon next to properties like **Position, Opacity, Scale,** or **Rotation**.

4. **Animate the Text**:

   - To animate, move the **Playhead** along the timeline, and adjust the **Position, Opacity,** or **Scale** at different points.

   - Photoshop will automatically create the in-between frames, smoothly transitioning the text between the keyframes.

5. **Adjust Timing and Easing**:

   - You can adjust the timing of the animation by moving the keyframes closer together or further apart.

   - Use the **Ease In** and **Ease Out** options to create smooth transitions between keyframes for more natural animations.

Text Animation Example:

Let's say you want to animate a **bouncing text** effect. Here's how you could do it:

- Create the text you want to animate.

- Set a starting keyframe with the **Position** property to place the text off-screen (below the frame).

- Add a second keyframe where the text comes into view and bounces back up (using the **Scale** and **Rotation** properties to make it bounce).

- Add easing to make the movement smooth and natural.

Adding Motion to Shapes and Images

Animating shapes or images involves the same basic principles as text animation. You can animate elements like logos, icons, or abstract shapes to create dynamic visual content.

How to Animate Shapes and Images:

1. **Import or Create Shapes**:

   - Use the **Shape Tool** to create basic shapes (rectangles, circles, polygons) or import images to use as layers in your composition.

2. **Convert to Video Layers**:

   - As with text, convert these shapes or images into video layers so they can be animated in the timeline.

3. **Add Keyframes and Animate**:

   - Add keyframes for properties such as **Position**, **Opacity**, and **Rotation**.

   - Move the elements across the screen, change their size, or make them disappear and reappear.

4. **Using the Puppet Warp Tool for Image Animation**:

   ○ For more complex animations, you can use the **Puppet Warp Tool** to manipulate parts of an image or shape. This tool allows you to add pins to areas of your image and move them like a puppet, creating fluid animations.

Animating Multiple Layers Simultaneously

You can animate multiple elements within your composition at once by linking them together or animating them independently. Photoshop allows you to animate several elements and synchronize their motion to create cohesive, professional animations.

Color Grading Video Clips in Photoshop

Color grading is one of the most significant parts of video editing. It enhances the overall atmosphere and look of your video and maintains visual consistency across different shots. Photoshop 2025 includes extensive color grading capabilities that allow you to change the hues and tones of your video footage, whether you are going for a cinematic look, vintage feel, or a current style.

What is Color Grading?

Color grading is the process of modifying the color balance, contrast, brightness, and saturation of a video. While color correction fixes faults with lighting or exposure, color grading enhances the artistic appeal of the video and produces a certain mood or ambiance.

How to Color Grade Video Clips in Photoshop 2025:

1. **Import the Video Clip**:

   ○ First, import the video clips into your Photoshop project. Open the **Timeline Panel** and select your video layer.

2. **Add an Adjustment Layer**:

   ○ Go to **Layer > New Adjustment Layer** and choose from options like **Hue/Saturation, Curves, Levels**, or **Color Lookup**.

   ○ These adjustment layers allow you to manipulate the colors and tones of your video clips non-destructively, so you can always go back and tweak the settings later.

3. **Adjust the Colors and Tones**:

   o **Hue/Saturation**: Use this adjustment to shift colors, desaturate, or intensify certain hues.

   o **Curves**: The **Curves** tool gives you precise control over the shadows, midtones, and highlights, allowing you to create a balanced or contrast-heavy look.

   o **Levels**: **Levels** adjust the exposure and contrast, correcting any underexposed or overexposed areas.

   o **Color Lookup**: The **Color Lookup** adjustment lets you apply cinematic color grading presets, giving your video a stylized look with ease.

4. **Apply LUTs (Look-Up Tables)**:

   o Photoshop 2025 allows you to apply **LUTs** (Look-Up Tables), which are pre-set color grades that give your video a specific visual style. You can find LUTs that mimic the colors of film stock, vintage photography, or modern cinematography.

   o Simply go to **Layer > New Adjustment Layer > Color Lookup** and choose a LUT from the dropdown menu. Adjust the intensity by modifying the **Opacity**.

5. **Fine-Tune Color Grading**:

   o You can further adjust the **contrast**, **saturation**, and **brightness** to refine the color grading and ensure that your video clips match the overall tone you want to achieve.

Creating Cinematic Looks

If you want to create a **cinematic** look, consider the following:

- **Reduce Contrast**: Cinematic videos often have softer contrasts, so use the **Curves** tool to reduce the highlights and shadows.

- **Add a Color Tint**: Apply a **blue** or **teal-orange** tint to your video using **Color Lookup** or **Hue/Saturation** for a modern look.

- **Vignette**: Add a subtle vignette to focus attention on the center of the frame by creating a **layer mask** with a soft **black gradient**.

Exporting Your Final Video Projects

After editing your video and adding animation, it's time to export your final video. Photoshop 2025 offers multiple export options for video content, depending on your project's needs—whether you're exporting a video for **social media**, **film production**, or **online platforms**.

How to Export Video Projects in Photoshop 2025:

1. **Finalize Your Timeline**:

   - Ensure that your video timeline is fully edited and all transitions, animations, and color grading have been applied.

   - Review your video one last time to make sure everything looks polished.

2. **Go to Export**:

   - Once you're ready to export, go to **File > Export > Render Video**.

3. **Choose Export Settings**:

   - **Format**: You can choose from various formats, including **H.264** (for MP4), **QuickTime**, or **GIF**.

   - **Preset**: Select a preset that best fits your project's purpose, such as **YouTube**, **HD 1080p**, or **1080p (for social media)**.

   - **Resolution**: Choose the resolution for your video. Make sure to match the resolution of your project (e.g., 1920x1080 for Full HD).

   - **Frame Rate**: Choose the appropriate frame rate for your video project. Standard options are **24 fps** for cinematic videos and **30 fps** for more general uses.

4. **Render the Video**:

   - Once you've adjusted the settings, click **Render** to export the video file. Photoshop will process the video and export it in the selected format.

5. **Save Your Work**:

   ○ After exporting, save your project as a **PSD** file in case you need to go back and make future changes. This ensures that all layers, adjustments, and keyframes are preserved for later use.

Project: Creating a Short Animated Video with Photoshop

Now that we've covered the essentials of **adding motion** to text, shapes, and images, **color grading**, and **exporting**, let's apply these skills in a practical project. In this project, we'll create a **short animated video** using the techniques discussed in this chapter.

Step 1: Setting Up Your Video Project

1. **Open a New Project**: Start by creating a new Photoshop document with a **1920x1080 px** canvas. Set the **resolution** to 72 dpi for video.

2. **Import Your Media**: Import any images, video clips, or graphics you want to animate. These might include backgrounds, logos, text, or other graphic elements.

Step 2: Animating the Text and Shapes

1. **Add Text**: Use the **Text Tool (T)** to create a title for your video, such as "Welcome to Photoshop 2025."

2. **Animate the Text**: Use **keyframes** to animate the text, having it appear from the bottom of the screen and move upward. Adjust **opacity** and **position** keyframes to create smooth transitions.

Step 3: Adding Motion to Graphics

1. **Add Shapes**: Use the **Shape Tool** to create a dynamic background or a logo animation.

2. **Animate the Shapes**: Use keyframes to animate their position and scale, making them move or grow during the animation.

Step 4: Color Grading the Video

1. **Apply Color Grading**: Use **Adjustment Layers** to enhance the color grading of your video. Add a **cool-toned color filter** for a sleek, modern feel.

2. **Fine-Tune with Curves**: Adjust the **Curves** layer to enhance contrast and depth, giving your video a polished cinematic look.

Step 5: Exporting the Video

1. **Review and Export**: Once your animation is complete, review the video to ensure all elements flow seamlessly. Export the final version as an **MP4 file** for high-quality playback.

Photoshop 2025's video editing and animation capabilities provide powerful tools to create professional-quality video material.

Whether you're adding motion to text, making dynamic forms, or working with color grading, Photoshop gives flexibility and creativity at every stage of the process.

With the techniques taught in this chapter, you can begin incorporating motion graphics into your workflow and elevate your video projects to the next level.

Chapter 10

Photoshop for Web and Graphic Design – Professional Workflows

Photoshop has always been a vital tool for graphic designers, and as the digital world continues to change, it stays at the vanguard of online and graphic design. Adobe Photoshop 2025 further cements its role as a powerful platform for developing web graphics, user interfaces (UI), and websites. With the increased emphasis on digital media for marketing, user experience (UX), and branding, designers must grasp Photoshop's abilities to create polished, professional designs that operate effectively across many platforms.

The web design market alone was worth over $40 billion in 2020, and it's predicted to rise annually by more than 8%. As this market continues to flourish, the demand for high-quality visuals, dynamic websites, and user-friendly interfaces also increases. For designers, knowing the workflow between Photoshop and other design and development technologies is crucial to staying competitive and addressing the different needs of clients and organizations.

In this chapter, we will investigate how Photoshop 2025 may be exploited to create amazing web graphics such as icons, banners, and page layouts, and we'll dive into recommended practices for preparing pictures for the web. Additionally, we will coach you through creating user interfaces (UI) and websites, ensuring your designs are visually appealing, functional, and optimized for the online.

Creating Web Graphics: Icons, Banners, and Layouts

When working with online design, web visuals are vital for developing interesting user experiences. Icons, banners, and layouts are crucial visual elements that not only convey a brand's identity but also facilitate navigation, engagement, and content consumption. Photoshop includes features that make developing these pieces straightforward and adaptable, allowing you to produce great visuals for any website or app.

Designing Icons for the online Icons are the building blocks of modern online design. They express fundamental concepts and actions—such as home, search, social media, or shopping carts—in a visually concise and intuitive style. In web design, icons must be clear, recognized, and scalable to multiple sizes.

How to Create Icons in Photoshop 2025:

1. **Start with a New Document**: Begin by creating a new document with a **transparent background**. Icons are usually designed in a **square canvas**, often sized at **512x512 pixels** for larger displays, but ultimately saved in **multiple sizes** for various screen resolutions.

2. **Use Vector Tools**: The **Shape Tool** (U) is perfect for creating clean, sharp edges for icons. Start with basic shapes (circles, squares, lines) and combine them to create more complex designs. Use the **Path Selection Tool** to adjust and refine the paths of your shapes.

3. **Use Layer Styles for Effects**: To add **depth** or **shadows** to your icons, use **Layer Styles** such as **Drop Shadow**, **Inner Glow**, or **Bevel & Emboss**. These effects can add dimension and make your icon more visually appealing on websites and apps.

4. **Simplify the Design**: Icons should be simple and clear, with minimal detail to ensure they are recognizable even at smaller sizes. Use the **Path Tool** (P) for more control over shapes and ensure all elements are vector-based to maintain clarity when resized.

5. **Save the Icon**: Once the icon is complete, save it in **SVG (Scalable Vector Graphics)** format for the highest quality and scalability. You can also save it as a **PNG** for use in web environments where transparency is required.

Designing Banners and Headers for Websites

Banners and headers are essential for grabbing attention and conveying the key message of a website. These large, visually impactful graphics often appear at the top of a website or within **landing pages**, and they can include call-to-action buttons, text, and imagery.

How to Create Banners in Photoshop 2025:

1. **Set Up the Canvas**: Start by creating a new document with the dimensions needed for your banner. Common banner sizes include **728x90 pixels** (leaderboard) and **300x250 pixels** (medium rectangle), but the dimensions will vary depending on the layout and device you are designing for.

2. **Add Background and Visual Elements**: Use high-quality images, gradients, or textures for the background. You can use **Layer Styles** to add effects such as a **gradient overlay** or **pattern fill** to create depth and interest.

3. **Typography and Call to Action**: Banners often include **text** with a call-to-action (CTA). Choose web-friendly fonts that are easy to read and match the branding of the website. Use **contrast** and **hierarchy** to highlight important text.

4. **Use Smart Objects for Scalability**: To ensure your banner looks great across various screen resolutions, convert key elements such as images or logos into **Smart Objects**. This allows you to resize the objects without losing quality.

5. **Save and Export**: When saving your banner, it is crucial to choose the appropriate format. **JPEG** is often the best choice for images, while **PNG** is ideal for banners with transparency. Use the **Save for Web** option to optimize file sizes for faster load times without compromising quality.

Designing Layouts for Web Pages

The layout of a web page is critical to its usability and aesthetic appeal. A well-organized layout can enhance user experience and engagement. When designing web page layouts, consider the **grid system**, **visual hierarchy**, and the **responsive nature** of modern websites.

How to Create Web Layouts in Photoshop 2025:

1. **Set Up a Grid System**: Begin by setting up a **grid system** to help organize your layout elements. Go to **View > Show > Grid** to display Photoshop's grid, which will help you align objects consistently. You can also create a **custom grid** by going to **Edit > Preferences > Guides, Grid & Slices**.

2. **Design the Header, Navigation, and Footer**: Use the **Shape Tool** and **Text Tool** to create the essential elements of the page layout, such as the **navigation bar**, **logo**, and **footer**. These elements will be present on every page, so it's important to ensure they are consistent across the design.

3. **Create Content Sections**: Design distinct content areas such as **hero sections**, **image galleries**, or **feature highlights**. You can use placeholder text and images to represent content and layout these sections with the grid system.

4. **Use Smart Objects for Reusability**: If certain elements, like logos or icons, are used across multiple pages, consider turning them into **Smart Objects** so you can reuse them without manually resizing or adjusting them each time.

5. **Exporting Web Layouts**: Save your layout as a **PSD** file to preserve layers and adjustments for future edits. When sharing or handing off the design to developers, export sections as **PNG** or **JPEG** files.

Preparing Images for the Web: File Formats and Optimization

Optimizing pictures for the web is crucial for guaranteeing fast loading times, better user experience, and enhanced SEO rankings. Photoshop 2025 offers a lot of options that let you alter the file format, resolution, and compression settings to find the ideal balance between image quality and performance.

Understanding File Formats for the Web

Different image formats are optimized for different uses on the web. Understanding when to use each format is essential for getting the best visual and performance results.

1. **JPEG**:

   o **Best for**: Photographs and complex images with many colors.

   o **Pros**: Small file size and wide support.

   o **Cons**: Lossy compression, which reduces image quality, especially when saving at lower quality settings.

2. **PNG**:

   o **Best for**: Images with transparency (e.g., logos, icons) and graphics with fewer colors.

   o **Pros**: Lossless compression, retaining image quality, and supporting transparency.

   o **Cons**: Larger file size compared to JPEG.

3. **GIF**:

   o **Best for**: Simple animations and images with a limited color palette (up to 256 colors).

- o **Pros**: Ideal for small animations, transparency support.

- o **Cons**: Limited color range, not suitable for high-quality images.

4. **SVG**:

- o **Best for**: Icons and logos that need to be scalable without losing quality.

- o **Pros**: Scalable without loss of quality, small file sizes.

- o **Cons**: Limited support for complex imagery and color gradients.

5. **WebP**:

- o **Best for**: High-quality images at smaller file sizes for use in websites.

- o **Pros**: High compression with minimal loss of quality, supports transparency.

- o **Cons**: Not universally supported across all browsers.

Optimizing Images for the Web

To ensure your images load quickly and retain their quality, it is important to properly optimize them. Photoshop's **Save for Web** feature helps you fine-tune the balance between image quality and file size.

How to Optimize Images for the Web:

1. **Use the 'Save for Web' Feature**:

   - o Go to **File > Export > Save for Web (Legacy)**. This opens a window where you can adjust image settings and see a live preview of the file size and image quality.

2. **Choose the Right Compression**:

   - o For **JPEGs**, adjust the quality slider to find the right balance between quality and file size. A setting around **60-80%** is usually a good balance for web images.

   - o For **PNGs**, choose the **PNG-8** format for simpler images (with fewer colors) and **PNG-24** for images with transparency or complex details.

3. **Rescale Images**:

   ○ Web images need to be resized appropriately to fit within the page layout. Use **Image > Image Size** to resize images to the correct dimensions for web use.

4. **Sharpen Images**:

   ○ When optimizing for the web, images can sometimes appear soft. Apply a subtle **Unsharp Mask** or **Smart Sharpen** to enhance details before exporting.

5. **Consider Responsive Design**:

   ○ When designing for responsive websites, consider creating multiple versions of the same image at different sizes to optimize for mobile, tablet, and desktop screens.

Designing User Interfaces (UI) and Websites

Photoshop is an immensely effective tool for developing user interfaces (UI) and websites. UI design focuses on the appearance and feel of the website or app, and it's all about creating an intuitive experience for the user. With Photoshop 2025, designers can develop high-fidelity wireframes, buttons, menus, and interactive elements that are ready for execution.

Designing User Interfaces (UI)

UI design entails building the items that users interact with, such as buttons, forms, navigation menus, and sliders. The goal is to ensure the interface is visually beautiful, functional, and easy to use.

How to Design UI Elements in Photoshop:

1. **Create a New Document**:

   ○ Set up a new document that matches the screen resolution of the device you're designing for. Common sizes include **1440x900 px** for desktop and **375x667 px** for mobile.

2. **Design Buttons and Icons**:

   ○ Use the **Shape Tool** to create buttons and icons. Add text, gradients, and subtle shadows to make the buttons look clickable and engaging.

   ○ Consider using **Layer Styles** like **Inner Glow** or **Bevel & Emboss** to give depth to buttons and icons.

3. **Design Navigation Menus**:

   ○ Design horizontal or vertical navigation bars with consistent fonts, colors, and alignment. Consider the **spacing** and **hierarchy** of menu items to ensure ease of use.

4. **Wireframes and Prototypes**:

   ○ Create wireframes to lay out the basic structure of your website or app before adding detailed graphics. Use simple shapes to represent content areas, buttons, and images.

   ○ Once the wireframe is approved, you can begin adding color, texture, and images to create a polished design.

5. **User Flow**:

   ○ Design **user flow diagrams** to visualize how users will interact with your interface. This helps identify any potential issues with navigation and improves the overall user experience.

Designing Websites

When designing a full website in Photoshop, it's essential to think about layout, visual hierarchy, and responsive design. While Photoshop is not a web development tool, it allows you to create static designs and deliver assets to developers for implementation.

How to Design Websites in Photoshop:

1. **Create a Web Layout**:

   - Use the **grid system** to lay out content such as headers, sidebars, and footer areas. Start with a standard **12-column grid** for flexibility.

2. **Use Smart Objects for Reusability**:

   - Convert repeated elements like **logos** and **icons** into **Smart Objects** for easy updates and resizing.

3. **Create a Responsive Design**:

   - Design for different screen sizes by creating separate layouts for desktop, tablet, and mobile views. Use the **Artboard Tool** to manage multiple layouts within the same file.

4. **Prototype the Interaction**:

   - Use Photoshop to design interactive elements like dropdown menus, hover effects, and modal windows. While you can't code interactions in Photoshop, you can visualize them for developers.

Vector Art for Print and Digital Media

Vector art is a vital tool in both print and digital media design, allowing designers to produce scalable visuals that keep great quality at any scale. Unlike raster images, which rely on pixels, vector graphics use mathematical equations to produce forms, lines, and colors, making them perfect for designs that need to be enlarged without loss of quality.

Photoshop 2025 continues to strengthen its handling of vector graphics, with better pen tools, shape tools, and path manipulation features, allowing you to produce detailed and scalable artwork for a multitude of tasks.

Benefits of Using Vector Art in Design:

- **Scalability**: Vector images can be resized infinitely without losing resolution, making them perfect for logos, icons, and illustrations.

- **File Size Efficiency**: Vector files are often smaller than high-resolution raster images, making them ideal for websites and digital applications where fast loading times are essential.

- **Precision**: Vector tools in Photoshop allow for pixel-perfect designs, especially when creating logos, illustrations, or other graphic elements that require accuracy.

Creating Vector Art in Photoshop 2025

1. **Using the Pen Tool for Precision**:

    - The **Pen Tool** (P) is Photoshop's primary tool for creating vector paths. These paths can be used to form intricate shapes, logos, or illustrations.

    - With the Pen Tool, you can click to create anchor points and drag to create curves. By adjusting the **Bezier curves**, you can achieve smooth, flowing shapes.

2. To use the Pen Tool:

    - Select the **Pen Tool** (P) from the **Tools Panel**.

    - Click to create **anchor points** and drag to manipulate the curves. Hold **Shift** while clicking to create straight lines.

    - To close a path, click on the initial anchor point.

3. **Working with Shape Tools**:

    - Photoshop also offers a wide variety of **vector shape tools**, including rectangles, ellipses, polygons, and custom shapes. These tools are essential for creating icons, logos, and other graphic elements.

    - To create a vector shape:

        - Select the **Shape Tool** (U) from the **Tools Panel**.

- Choose the desired shape and drag to draw it on the canvas. You can adjust its size and fill color as needed.

4. **Editing Paths and Shapes**:

   - Once you've created paths or shapes, you can **edit** them using the **Path Selection Tool** (A) or **Direct Selection Tool** (A). These tools let you manipulate anchor points, curves, and segments of paths to refine your design.

   - You can also apply **stroke styles** and **fill options** to the paths to give them depth and dimension.

5. **Converting to Smart Objects for Scalability**:

   - When you finish creating your vector design, you can convert it to a **Smart Object**. This allows you to scale it without loss of quality and apply non-destructive editing later on.

6. **Exporting Vector Art**:

   - Once your vector artwork is ready, you can save it in **AI**, **SVG**, or **PDF** formats for use in print or digital media.

   - For web use, you can export the vector graphic as an **SVG** file, which maintains scalability while being lightweight for faster website load times.

Advanced Typography in Graphic Design

Typography is one of the most effective tools in graphic design. It has the capacity to transmit emotion, meaning, and identity through the careful selection of typefaces, letter-spacing, alignment, and color. In Photoshop 2025, the Text Tool has been upgraded with more possibilities for producing and styling text, allowing you to take your typographic creations to new heights.

Understanding Typography in Graphic Design

Typography is more than just choosing a typeface. It's about the visual arrangement of text and how it interacts with other aspects in the design. Effective typography makes text readable, beautiful, and cohesive with the overall design. Whether you're developing a website header, poster, or brand identity, understanding typography's significance in your designs is vital.

Advanced Typography Techniques in Photoshop 2025:

1. **Using Paragraph and Character Styles**:

    o   Photoshop 2025 allows you to create and apply **paragraph** and **character styles** to text layers. These styles help you maintain consistent typography throughout your design.

    o   **Character Styles** let you control the font, size, leading, kerning, and color of individual characters.

    o   **Paragraph Styles** allow you to set alignment, indentation, and spacing between paragraphs. These features are essential for maintaining uniformity in large design projects.

2. **Text Effects and Layer Styles**:

    o   Photoshop offers a variety of **layer styles** that can be applied to text, such as **drop shadows**, **glows**, **bevels**, and **embossing**. These effects add depth and dimension to text and make it stand out in your design.

    o   You can use the **Layer Styles** panel to add and adjust these effects. To create a more dramatic typography effect, consider using **gradient overlays** or **pattern fills**.

3. **Working with Text on Paths**:

    o   One of the most unique features of Photoshop for typography is the ability to create **text on paths**. You can add text along **curves**, **shapes**, or even custom paths you've created using the **Pen Tool**.

    o   To add text on a path:

        ■   Create a path using the **Pen Tool** (P).

        ■   Select the **Text Tool** (T) and click on the path. The cursor will change to indicate that text can be placed along the path.

- Type your text, and Photoshop will automatically align it along the path. You can adjust the **text flow** and position as needed.

4. **Typographic Composition for Web and Print**:

   ○ **Typography for web**: When designing for the web, always consider **web-safe fonts** or **Google Fonts** to ensure your text displays consistently across devices and browsers.

   ○ **Typography for print**: When designing for print, consider the physical dimensions of the print product, such as a business card, flyer, or brochure. You can use **photoshop's guides and rulers** to properly align and scale text for print layouts.

5. **Typography for Branding**:

   ○ The use of typography in branding helps establish a company's identity. In Photoshop, you can combine **text**, **shapes**, and **colors** to create custom **typographic logos** and **brand names**.

Working with Smart Objects and Linked Files

Smart Objects and linked files are vital for non-destructive editing in Photoshop, especially when working on big design projects that contain several aspects. These features enable you to keep flexibility in your process, making it easier to update and adjust assets as your design evolves.

What Are Smart Objects?

A Smart Object is a container that houses one or more layers or images. Unlike ordinary layers, Smart Objects maintain the original data of the image, allowing you to manipulate it without permanently affecting the image. This means you may scale, rotate, and manipulate the object without sacrificing quality or resolution.

How to Use Smart Objects in Photoshop 2025:

1. **Convert Layers to Smart Objects**:

   - To convert a layer into a Smart Object, **right-click** on the layer and choose **Convert to Smart Object**.

   - Once converted, you can double-click the Smart Object thumbnail to edit its contents in a separate window. The original layer data is preserved, and any transformations applied to the Smart Object will be non-destructive.

2. **Non-Destructive Editing**:

   - With **Smart Filters**, you can apply filters (such as blur, sharpen, or distort) to Smart Objects and then modify or remove them later without affecting the original image data.

   - This is perfect for projects where you need to test different effects or make revisions without permanently altering the original artwork.

Linked Files for Efficient Workflow

When working on large projects or collaborating with others, it's common to work with **linked files**. Linked files allow you to reference external images or assets in your Photoshop document, rather than embedding them directly.

1. **Using Linked Files**:

   - When you place an image in Photoshop using **File > Place Linked**, Photoshop creates a reference to the original file, rather than embedding the image within the PSD. This reduces the overall file size of the document and allows you to update the image externally without opening Photoshop.

2. **Updating Linked Files**:

   - If the linked file is updated, Photoshop will automatically reflect the changes when you open the document. This is extremely useful for working with assets that change frequently, such as logos, product images, or marketing materials.

Project: Designing a Website Header and Icon Set

Now that we've covered the key design concepts in Photoshop for web and graphic design, let's apply them in a practical project: designing a **website header** and an **icon set**. In this project, we will focus on using **vector shapes**, **typography**, **smart objects**, and **linked files** to create a cohesive set of web graphics.

Step 1: Set Up the Canvas and Guidelines

1. **Create a New Document**: Start by setting up a new document with the following dimensions:

   - **Website Header**: 1920x300 px

   - **Icon Set**: 500x500 px (for each icon)

2. **Add Guidelines**: Set up **guidelines** for precise alignment of your text, images, and icons. Use **View > New Guide** to create vertical and horizontal guides.

Step 2: Designing the Website Header

1. **Add Background and Color**: Use a **gradient fill** or a **pattern overlay** for the background. Consider using **layer styles** to add texture or a subtle shadow.

2. **Typography**: Use the **Text Tool** to create the website's name or title. Apply appropriate **font** choices, **kerning**, and **letter-spacing** to ensure the text is balanced and easy to read.

3. **Add Logo or Icons**: Import your logo or icons and place them on the header. Convert them to **Smart Objects** to allow for easy resizing and adjustments.

4. **Add a Call to Action**: Create a call-to-action (CTA) button with text and a **gradient effect** to make it stand out.

Step 3: Designing the Icon Set

1. **Choose Simple Shapes**: Use **vector shapes** to create icons like **home**, **search**, or **settings**. Keep the designs simple and consistent.

2. **Typography**: Use a small **iconography font** for text-based icons (e.g., **Font Awesome**). Ensure the font is legible even at small sizes.

3. **Color Palette**: Stick to a limited color palette for consistency. You can use **Layer Styles** to add **shadows** or **glows** for emphasis.

Step 4: Exporting the Web Graphics

1. **Export the Website Header**: Save the header as a **JPEG** or **PNG**. If the header includes transparency, use **PNG** format to preserve the transparent background.

2. **Export the Icon Set**: Export each icon as a **PNG** with a transparent background. Ensure the resolution is set to **72dpi** for web use.

Photoshop 2025 is a vital tool for web and graphic design. With its extensive tools for vector graphics, complex typography, smart objects, and connected files, designers can create beautiful, functional, and optimized designs for both print and digital media.

By following expert workflows and mastering these strategies, you'll be well on your way to designing amazing visuals that stand out on websites, applications, and digital platforms.

In this chapter, we've explored how to design icons, banners, and web layouts, optimize photos for the web, and work with UI design elements. You've also learnt how to streamline your process by employing smart objects and connected files for effective design.

Chapter 11

Advanced Photoshop Techniques – Unlocking the Full Potential of Your Creativity

As a creative expert, Photoshop 2025 provides you a plethora of tools and features that go far beyond basic photo alteration. While it's recognized for its picture editing capabilities, Photoshop also empowers you to automate operations, build custom pieces, and speed up your workflow with sophisticated techniques. Whether you're a designer, photographer, or digital artist, understanding how to leverage the full potential of Photoshop's advanced capabilities will substantially boost your productivity and creative output.

According to Adobe, actions and automation capabilities in Photoshop can cut repetitive activities by up to 75%, freeing up important time for more creative endeavors. The ability to automate workflows, create custom brushes, and generate patterns can improve your work, enabling you to focus more on the artistic parts of your projects.

The Power of Actions and Scripts

One of the most powerful and time-saving features in Photoshop is Actions. Actions allow you to record a set of commands and apply them to different files with a single click. Whether you're editing several pictures, applying specialized effects, or automating repetitive operations, Actions help you save time and maintain consistency across your projects.

What Are Actions in Photoshop?

An Action in Photoshop is essentially a sequence of commands, including tool selections, layer edits, filters, and transformations, that you may record and playback at any time.

This lets you apply complicated effects or edits to many photographs with the touch of a mouse. Actions may be particularly handy when you need to repeat a set of processes across a group of photos, such as resizing, cropping, or color correcting.

How to Record and Use Actions:

1. **Recording Actions**:

   o Open Photoshop and go to **Window > Actions** to display the **Actions panel**.

   o To create a new action, click the **New Action** button at the bottom of the panel. You will be prompted to name your action and assign it a function key if desired for quick access.

   o Once you click **Record**, Photoshop will start recording every action you perform, from adjusting layers to applying filters or creating selections.

   o When you're finished recording, click the **Stop** button in the Actions panel. Now, your action is saved and can be applied to other images.

2. **Applying Actions**:

   o To apply a recorded action, open the file you want to edit, select the action from the **Actions panel**, and click **Play**. Photoshop will automatically execute the series of steps recorded in that action.

   o Actions can also be customized by adding more steps after recording, or by editing existing steps if you need to fine-tune the process.

Common Uses of Actions:

- **Batch Processing**: Apply the same editing steps (e.g., resizing, watermarking) to a batch of photos.

- **Social Media Previews**: Automatically resize images for specific social media platforms like Instagram, Facebook, or Twitter.

- **Creative Effects**: Create effects that involve multiple steps, like applying a texture overlay, adjusting contrast, or adding filters.

- **Retouching**: Speed up the process of portrait retouching by automating the frequency separation or skin smoothing steps.

Using Scripts for More Complex Automation

While **Actions** are great for simple tasks, **Scripts** allow you to automate more complex workflows. Scripts are essentially small programs or scripts written in **JavaScript** that perform a series of commands based on parameters you set. Photoshop comes with a set of built-in scripts, and you can also create your own.

How to Use Scripts in Photoshop:

1. **Running Built-in Scripts**:

   ○ To run a script, go to **File > Scripts** and select a built-in script such as **Image Processor** or **Load Files into Stack**.

   ○ These scripts help with common tasks like batch processing images, renaming files, or automatically arranging layers.

2. **Writing Your Own Scripts**:

   ○ If you're comfortable with JavaScript, you can write custom scripts to automate specific processes. For example, you could write a script that automatically arranges layers in a specific order, renames files based on metadata, or even adjusts the exposure of photos in a batch.

   ○ Scripts can be saved as .jsx files, and you can run them from the **Scripts** menu by selecting **File > Scripts > Browse**.

Automating Your Workflow with Batch Processing

Batch processing is one of the most powerful techniques to automate your workflow and save time when working with several photos. Instead of manually applying an action to each image, you may automate the process for a full folder of files, assuring consistency and speed. Photoshop's batch processing tools allow you to apply a predetermined operation to several files in one go.

How to Set Up Batch Processing in Photoshop 2025

1. **Create Your Action**:

   ○ Before using batch processing, you need to create an action that you want to apply to multiple files. This could include resizing images, converting to black and white, or applying a watermark.

2. **Open the Batch Processing Dialogue**:

   ○ Go to **File > Automate > Batch** to open the **Batch** dialog box. In this window, you will set the source folder (where the images are located) and the destination folder (where you want to save the processed images).

3. **Choose the Action**:

   ○ Under **Action**, select the action you created earlier. This action will be applied to each file in the selected source folder.

4. **Set File Naming Conventions**:

   ○ You can specify naming conventions for the exported files under the **File Naming** section, allowing you to automatically rename the processed files based on specific criteria (e.g., adding a suffix or prefix to the original filename).

5. **Set Destination Folder**:

   ○ Choose where you want to save the processed files. You can save them in the original location or specify a new folder.

6. **Run the Batch**:

   ○ Once all the settings are configured, click **OK** to begin the batch process. Photoshop will automatically open each file, apply the action, and save the result in the designated folder.

Batch processing is incredibly useful for tasks like resizing a set of images for web use, applying a filter to multiple photos, or adjusting the exposure of an entire image collection.

Creating and Using Custom Brushes and Patterns

One of the most creative and personalized capabilities of Photoshop is the ability to create custom brushes and patterns. These tools allow you to add texture, detail, and style to your artwork, making your designs distinctive and personalized to your needs.

Creating Custom Brushes in Photoshop 2025

Custom brushes may replicate a broad variety of effects, from painting textures to adding complex details like hair strands or fabric patterns. Photoshop's brush engine is highly powerful, enabling you to design brushes that match your particular requirements.

How to Create a Custom Brush:

1. **Create the Brush Source**:

   o Start by creating an image or shape that you want to turn into a brush. This could be a simple black-and-white design or a more complex texture.

   o For example, you can create a grunge texture, a leaf shape, or a hand-drawn sketch.

2. **Define the Brush**:

   o Select the shape or texture and go to **Edit > Define Brush Preset**. This will convert your selected shape into a brush.

   o Name your new brush and click **OK**.

3. **Customize Brush Settings**:

   o Once the brush is created, you can modify its settings by going to the **Brush Settings Panel** (Window > Brush Settings). Here, you can adjust parameters like:

   ▪ **Spacing**: Controls the distance between brush strokes.

   ▪ **Shape Dynamics**: Adjusts the size, angle, and roundness of the brush based on pressure or tilt.

   ▪ **Texture**: Adds textures to the brush strokes.

- **Dual Brush**: Combines two brushes to create complex patterns and effects.

4. **Use the Brush**:

   ○ Once your brush is customized, select it from the **Brush Tool (B)** and start painting on your canvas. The new brush will behave according to the settings you've applied.

Creating Custom Patterns in Photoshop 2025

Patterns are a great way to add repeating designs, textures, or backgrounds to your work. You can create custom patterns from images, textures, or shapes, and use them as fills in your designs.

How to Create a Custom Pattern:

1. **Create the Pattern**:

   ○ Start by creating a design or texture that you want to use as a pattern. It should be a **seamless design**, meaning it can tile without showing visible edges when repeated.

2. **Define the Pattern**:

   ○ Select the area of the design you want to use as the pattern and go to **Edit > Define Pattern**. Name the pattern and click **OK**.

3. **Apply the Pattern**:

   ○ To use the pattern, create a new layer, select the **Paint Bucket Tool (G)**, and choose **Pattern** as the fill option. Click to fill the layer with your custom pattern.

   ○ You can also apply the pattern using a **Pattern Fill Layer** for non-destructive editing.

Project: Designing a Website Header and Icon Set

In this project, we will apply the techniques covered in this chapter by designing a **website header** and an **icon set** using advanced Photoshop tools. This will include creating **custom brushes**, **patterns**, and using **actions** for optimization.

Step 1: Set Up the Canvas

1. **Create the Header**:

   o Start by creating a new document for the website header, typically sized at **1920 x 500 pixels**.

2. **Create Background with Patterns**:

   o Use a custom pattern for the background of the header. You can use a **subtle texture** or **geometric pattern** to add depth to the design.

Step 2: Design Icons

1. **Create Icons Using Custom Brushes**:

   o Create simple icons (e.g., home, search, settings) using **custom brushes** for texture and details.

   o Use the **Shape Tool** and **Pen Tool** to create base shapes, then refine them with your custom brushes.

Step 3: Save Time with Actions

1. **Automate Icon Resizing**:

   o Create an **Action** to automatically resize the icons to multiple formats for various devices (e.g., desktop, tablet, and mobile versions).

Step 4: Export for Web

1. **Optimize and Export**:

   o Once the header and icons are complete, use the **Save for Web** option to export them in appropriate formats (e.g., **JPEG** for the header, **PNG** for the icons).

Advanced Masking: Using Channels and Selections in New Ways

Masking is a fundamental method in Photoshop, enabling you to work non-destructively and mix diverse parts flawlessly. While basic masking includes utilizing layer masks to hide or show elements of a layer, sophisticated masking techniques—especially with channels and selections—offer significantly more control over the minute aspects of your compositions. These methods are critical for jobs like carving out complex forms, mixing textures, and making exact edges.

What Are Channels and How Do They Work for Masking?

Channels are essentially grayscale images that store information about the colors in your image. Photoshop automatically creates three channels for RGB (Red, Green, and Blue) color images, plus an additional Alpha Channel for any alpha (transparency) information. Each channel has varied levels of information about the brightness of each pixel, and you may utilize this data to generate exact masks.

Using Channels for Masking:

1. **View the Channels Panel**:

   ○ Open the **Channels Panel** by going to **Window > Channels**. Here you will see individual channels for the **Red**, **Green**, and **Blue** components of your image.

2. **Create a New Channel for Masking**:

   ○ If your image has high contrast between the subject and the background, select the channel with the most contrast (often the **Blue Channel**). Press **Ctrl + A** (Windows) or **Cmd + A** (Mac) to select the entire channel, then **Ctrl + C** or **Cmd + C** to copy it.

3. **Create a Selection from the Channel**:

   ○ Paste the copied channel into a new alpha channel. This will be used as the base for your mask. You can use **Image > Adjustments > Levels** or **Curves** to increase the contrast and fine-tune the mask's detail.

4. **Apply the Channel Mask**:

   o Once you're satisfied with the contrast, **Ctrl + click** (Windows) or **Cmd + click** (Mac) on the thumbnail of the alpha channel to load the selection. Then, go to your original image and add a **Layer Mask**. This will apply the selection as a mask to the image.

This method is particularly useful for masking out complex backgrounds or subjects with fine details, such as **hair** or **feathers**, where other selection tools might struggle.

Refining Selections with the Quick Selection Tool and Refine Edge

After you create an initial selection, you often need to refine it to ensure the edges are sharp and smooth, particularly for intricate subjects like **portraits** or **hair**. Photoshop 2025 offers advanced tools like **Quick Selection** and **Refine Edge** to give you precise control over your selections.

1. **Quick Selection Tool**:

   o Use the **Quick Selection Tool (W)** to paint over the areas you want to include or exclude in the selection. Photoshop will automatically refine the selection based on the pixels you brush over, making it easier to select even the most complex areas.

2. **Refine Edge**:

   o Once a selection is made, go to **Select > Select and Mask**. In this workspace, you can use the **Refine Edge Brush Tool** to fine-tune areas like hair, fur, or soft edges. Adjust the **Radius** and **Smooth** sliders to clean up any imperfections in the selection.

By combining **channels** with these advanced selection tools, you can achieve **highly accurate and clean masks** for any project.

Creating Realistic Effects with 3D Tools and Textures

Photoshop's 3D capabilities have been continuously enhanced to allow designers to produce beautiful realistic effects, textures, and 3D models. Whether you're adding 3D pieces to a scene or generating textures that approximate depth and dimension, Photoshop provides strong tools for combining 3D items with 2D artwork.

Working with 3D Tools in Photoshop 2025

Photoshop 2025 adds even more powerful features for dealing with 3D models, letting you apply lighting, texturing, and shading with ease. Here's how you can make realistic effects with 3D tools:

Creating and Manipulating 3D Objects:

1. **Create a 3D Shape**:

   ○ Go to **3D > New 3D Layer from Selected Path** to create a 3D object from a vector shape. You can use **Photoshop's Shape Tools** to design the base of your 3D object, such as cubes, spheres, or more complex geometric shapes.

2. **Manipulate 3D Layers**:

   ○ Photoshop allows you to manipulate 3D objects using the **3D Panel**. You can **rotate**, **scale**, and **position** the 3D object in the workspace. Use the **3D tools** to adjust the **perspective** and add depth to your design.

3. **Apply 3D Textures and Materials**:

   ○ To make your 3D object look more realistic, apply **textures** or **materials**. Photoshop offers several pre-made materials, or you can use your own textures. Select the **3D Material** you want to apply and drag it onto your object in the 3D panel.

4. **Lighting Effects**:

   ○ Adjust the **lighting** of your 3D object by adding light sources such as **spotlights**, **point lights**, or **ambient lights**. Use the **3D Panel** to position and adjust the intensity of each light, creating shadows and highlights that give your object more realism.

5. **Rendering the 3D Model**:

   ○ Once the 3D object is positioned and textured, you can render it by going to **3D > Render**. This process applies the lighting and textures to create a realistic 3D model that can be integrated into your design.

Adding Realistic Textures to Your 2D Artwork

Photoshop's **texturing tools** allow you to add lifelike details to any 2D image. By combining **filters** and **3D textures**, you can create effects such as **grunge**, **metal**, **fabric**, or even **natural surfaces** like wood or stone.

How to Add Realistic Textures:

1. **Create a New Layer for Textures**:

   o Open or create the image you want to texture. Use the **Shape Tool** or **Pen Tool** to create areas for applying texture.

2. **Import a Texture**:

   o Find or create a texture that suits your design. Textures like **grunge**, **wood**, **stone**, and **fabric** can be applied to the new layer. You can either import a texture from your own library or find free textures online.

3. **Apply the Texture**:

   o Once your texture is imported, change the **blending mode** of the texture layer to something like **Overlay** or **Multiply**. Adjust the **opacity** to control how the texture blends with your original image.

4. **Adjust with Filters**:

   o Use filters like **Gaussian Blur** or **Noise** to fine-tune the texture and make it look more natural. You can also use the **Displace** filter to wrap textures around the surface of your 3D objects for even more realism.

By combining **3D models** with realistic textures and lighting, you can create designs that feel immersive and lifelike.

Experimenting with the Filter Gallery and Custom Filters

The Filter Gallery and custom filters are powerful tools in Photoshop that allow you to apply creative effects to your artwork, images, and projects. The Filter Gallery is a collection of pre-designed effects that you can apply with a single click, while custom filters enable you to create unique effects according to your design demands.

Using the Filter Gallery in Photoshop 2025

The Filter Gallery offers a wide variety of effects, from artistic and blur effects to distortions and texture simulations. The key to using the Filter Gallery effectively is experimenting with different settings and combinations to create a unique style for your artwork.

How to Use the Filter Gallery:

1. **Open the Filter Gallery**:

   ○ Go to **Filter > Filter Gallery** to access the wide range of built-in filters available in Photoshop. You can find filters organized by categories like **Artistic**, **Brush Strokes**, **Sketch**, and more.

2. **Apply a Filter**:

   ○ Choose a filter that suits your design. For example, the **Oil Paint** filter gives your image a brush stroke texture, while the **Watercolor** filter creates a soft, blended look. Adjust the settings to achieve the desired effect.

3. **Combine Multiple Filters**:

   ○ You can apply multiple filters to a single image by selecting **Add Filter** at the bottom of the gallery. This allows you to stack different effects for a more complex look.

Creating Custom Filters for Unique Effects

Creating custom filters in Photoshop allows you to generate one-of-a-kind effects that reflect your artistic style. You can create custom filters by combining different settings and applying them to your images or text.

How to Create Custom Filters:

1. **Create a New Layer for Effects**:

   ○ Start by creating a new layer or selecting the layer you want to apply the custom filter to.

2. **Apply the Filter**:

   ○ Go to **Filter > Other > Custom** to open the **Custom Filter** settings. Adjust the **radius**, **strength**, and other settings to create a unique effect.

3. **Use Adjustment Layers**:

    o   For more flexibility, combine custom filters with **adjustment layers** such as **Curves**, **Hue/Saturation**, or **Levels** to enhance the effect and make it more personalized.

Project: Designing a Complex Multi-Layered Artwork

Now that we've explored advanced techniques like **masking**, **3D effects**, and **filters**, let's bring it all together in a hands-on project. In this project, we'll create a **complex multi-layered artwork** that incorporates **advanced masking**, **realistic textures**, and **custom filters**.

Step 1: Set Up the Canvas

1. **Create a New Document**:

    o   Set up a new document with a large canvas size (e.g., **3000x2000 px**) to allow for detailed design work.

2. **Add Background and Texture**:

    o   Use a **gradient fill** or **texture pattern** for the background. You can add a **grunge texture** or use a **3D texture** for added depth.

Step 2: Import and Mask Elements

1. **Import Images**:

    o   Import different elements such as **portrait photos**, **objects**, or **illustrations**. Place them on separate layers for easy editing.

2. **Create Masks**:

    o   Use **advanced masking** techniques with channels to remove the background from the photos and ensure seamless integration with the textured background.

Step 3: Add 3D Effects and Realistic Lighting

1. **Apply 3D Elements**:

    o   Add a 3D object (e.g., a floating sphere or geometric shape) to your design. Use the **3D Panel** to position, scale, and texture the object.

2. **Lighting Effects**:

   ○ Use **spotlights** or **ambient light** to cast realistic shadows on the 3D object, ensuring it blends naturally with the 2D elements.

Step 4: Apply Custom Filters and Final Touches

1. **Experiment with Filters**:

   ○ Use the **Filter Gallery** to apply artistic effects or texture simulations to your artwork.

2. **Finalize with Custom Filters**:

   ○ Create **custom filters** to add finishing touches, such as a **painted look** or a subtle **grain effect**.

Step 5: Export the Artwork

1. **Save the PSD**:

   ○ Save your multi-layered artwork as a **PSD file** to preserve all layers and adjustments.

2. **Export for Web or Print**:

   ○ Export the final piece as a **JPEG** for web use or a **TIFF** for print, adjusting the resolution and quality to suit your needs.

In this chapter, we've studied how to harness the full power of Photoshop 2025 by learning sophisticated masking, generating realistic 3D effects, playing with the Filter Gallery, and developing complex, multi-layered artwork.

These advanced techniques give you the skills to take your creativity to the next level, whether you're working on digital art, graphic design, or photo modification.

By combining masking, texturing, and custom filters, you can create complicated, high-quality graphics that reflect your artistic vision. The skills and strategies gained here will help you streamline your workflow, giving you more time to focus on the creative parts of your projects.

Chapter 12

Photoshop Workflow Optimization - Speeding Up Your Work Process

In the fast-paced world of graphic design, picture editing, and digital art, time is frequently the most valuable asset. As projects expand in complexity, being organized and working efficiently is crucial to preserving quality while meeting deadlines. Adobe Photoshop 2025, as the industry-standard tool for creative professionals, offers significant tools to streamline workflows, automate repetitive operations, and enable for faster, more efficient design processes.

Did you realize that time efficiency is one of the main elements impacting creativity? According to a survey performed by Adobe, creative professionals report wasting up to 40% of their time on repetitive tasks that could be automated or optimized. With Photoshop 2025, you can regain that lost time by mastering workflow efficiency strategies like file and layer organization, batch processing, and keyboard shortcuts.

In this chapter, we will dive into real methods and tools that will help you work smarter, not harder. We'll cover how to organize your files and layers efficiently, automate jobs with Actions, Droplets, and Batch Processing, and speed up your day-to-day editing with keyboard shortcuts and custom hotkeys.

By the end of this chapter, you will be equipped with the knowledge to speed up your workflow, keep organized, and ultimately become more productive in Photoshop.

Organizing Your Files and Layers Efficiently

When working on intricate designs or picture alterations, maintaining your files and layers becomes vital. A well-organized file structure and layer management system not only makes the editing process smoother but also enables for easy changes and cooperation. With the extra complexity of dealing with various elements, Photoshop 2025 includes new features to help you stay organized, making your workflow as effective as possible.

The Importance of File Organization

arranging your project files is equally as crucial as arranging your layers in Photoshop. A well-structured file system can make your job more straightforward, especially when interacting with clients or team members. It helps eliminate misunderstanding, reduces time spent searching for files, and assures that you can find and change any piece of your project quickly.

Best Practices for Organizing Files:

1. **Create Folder Structures**:

    o   Use clear, descriptive folder names for your project. For example:

        ▪   **01_Assets** (for images, icons, textures)

        ▪   **02_Design** (for the working files)

        ▪   **03_Exports** (for final versions of files ready for delivery)

        ▪   **04_References** (for mood boards, inspiration, or client notes)

    o   Keep all assets used in the project within the project folder to maintain a clean workflow.

2. **Use Layer Folders and Groups**:

    o   Photoshop allows you to group layers within **Layer Folders**. For complex compositions, group related layers into folders, such as "**Background**", "**Main Elements**", or "**Text**".

    o   This not only keeps the **Layer Panel** clean but also makes it easier to locate and edit specific layers. To create a group, select multiple layers and press **Ctrl + G** (Windows) or **Cmd + G** (Mac).

3. **Name Your Layers**:

    o   Name your layers descriptively. For example, instead of "Layer 1", name it "Main Text" or "Background Image". This will save you time when navigating through a complex design, especially when you need to find a specific element quickly.

4. **Color Coding Layers**:

    o   Photoshop 2025 offers **layer color coding**. You can right-click on a layer and assign a color to it. This feature is useful when you have many layers to distinguish between different sections of your design (e.g., a **green label** for background elements and **blue for text**).

5. **Using Smart Objects**:

   ○ When you need to reuse elements such as logos, graphics, or patterns, converting them to **Smart Objects** ensures that they are non-destructive and can be easily updated. This also reduces file size and helps maintain consistency throughout your design.

6. **Version Control**:

   ○ It's a good practice to save multiple versions of your project, especially during major revisions. Use a version naming convention such as "**Project_v1**", "**Project_v2**", and so on, to ensure that you can easily track progress and revert to previous versions if needed.

How to Use the Layers Panel Efficiently:

1. **Layer Masks**:

   ○ Use **layer masks** for non-destructive editing. This allows you to hide or reveal parts of a layer without permanently deleting any content. Layer masks also enable you to create smooth transitions between layers, essential for compositing images or creating photo effects.

2. **Adjustment Layers**:

   ○ Always use **adjustment layers** for edits like brightness, contrast, saturation, and hue. These allow you to tweak your edits at any time, without affecting the original image data. You can apply multiple adjustments non-destructively and keep the changes flexible.

3. **Layer Styles**:

   ○ Layer styles like **drop shadows**, **inner glows**, and **stroke effects** can add depth to your designs. Apply these styles to entire groups of layers, or individual elements, to create unique effects with just a few clicks.

One of the most effective elements for workflow optimization in Photoshop 2025 is its automation capabilities. Actions, Droplets, and Batch Processing help you to automate repetitive activities, saving you time and lowering the risks of error. Whether you're altering many pictures, resizing materials for a website, or applying a set of effects throughout your designs, Photoshop makes it easy to streamline the process.

Using Actions to Automate Tasks

An Action is a recorded series of steps in Photoshop that you can play again with one click. You can construct your own actions to automate operations you do frequently, such as resizing photographs, altering brightness, or applying watermarks.

How to Create and Use Actions:

1. **Record an Action**:

   - To record a new action, open the **Actions Panel** (Window > Actions), then click on the **New Action** button. Name your action and choose a function key for quick access.

   - Press **Record** and perform the actions you want to automate, such as resizing, cropping, applying filters, or adjusting settings.

   - Once you finish, press **Stop** in the Actions panel. Now, you can play back this action whenever you need to apply the same steps.

2. **Play Back an Action**:

   - To use an action, select it from the **Actions Panel** and click **Play**. The action will be applied automatically to the active layer or document.

3. **Batch Process with Actions**:

   - You can use actions in conjunction with **Batch Processing** to apply the same steps to multiple images at once. This is a great way to apply uniform edits to a series of photos, such as resizing for web use or converting file formats.

Using Droplets for More Flexibility

Droplets are mini applications that allow you to run Photoshop actions on images outside of the program. Droplets are ideal for quickly applying actions to files without opening Photoshop, making them perfect for batch processing large numbers of files.

How to Create and Use Droplets:

1. **Create a Droplet**:

    ○   To create a droplet, go to **File > Automate > Create Droplet**. In the dialog box, choose the action you want to associate with the droplet.

    ○   Select the location to save the droplet, and customize the options for handling files (such as saving to a specific folder or applying certain naming conventions).

2. **Using the Droplet**:

    ○   To use the droplet, simply drag and drop files or folders onto the droplet icon. The associated action will be applied automatically to the files.

Batch Processing Multiple Files

Batch processing allows you to apply an action to an entire folder of files, which is especially useful when working with large volumes of images or assets. Here's how you can set up batch processing in Photoshop:

How to Use Batch Processing:

1. **Set Up the Batch Process**:

    ○   Go to **File > Automate > Batch** to open the batch dialog. Select the source folder containing the files you want to edit.

    ○   Choose the action you wish to apply to the images and set the destination folder for saving the processed files.

2. **Customize Batch Settings**:

    ○   You can adjust settings such as file naming conventions, file format options (JPEG, PNG, TIFF), and resolution. Photoshop will automatically apply the selected action to each file in the source folder and save the results in the destination folder.

Batch processing is ideal for tasks like resizing images, applying filters, or saving files in different formats.

Speeding Up Your Workflow with Keyboard Shortcuts and Custom Hotkeys

Mastering keyboard shortcuts is one of the quickest and most efficient ways to speed up your workflow in Photoshop. Photoshop comes with a large number of preset shortcuts that help you access tools and functionalities fast. Additionally, you can set custom hotkeys for activities, tools, and tasks that you use most frequently.

Default Keyboard Shortcuts:

Photoshop 2025 has a host of default shortcuts designed to streamline your workflow. Here are a few essential shortcuts every designer and photographer should know:

- **Ctrl + N (Windows) / Cmd + N (Mac)**: New Document

- **Ctrl + S (Windows) / Cmd + S (Mac)**: Save

- **Ctrl + Z (Windows) / Cmd + Z (Mac)**: Undo (Press multiple times for history states)

- **B**: Brush Tool

- **V**: Move Tool

- **M**: Marquee Tool

- **Ctrl + T (Windows) / Cmd + T (Mac)**: Free Transform

- **Ctrl + D (Windows) / Cmd + D (Mac)**: Deselect

- **Shift + Ctrl + N (Windows) / Shift + Cmd + N (Mac)**: New Layer

Creating Custom Keyboard Shortcuts:

To further enhance your productivity, you can create **custom keyboard shortcuts** for tools or functions that you use frequently. For example, if you often use the **Clone Stamp Tool** or **Layer Styles**, assigning a custom shortcut can save you time.

How to Customize Keyboard Shortcuts:

1. **Go to Edit > Keyboard Shortcuts:**

   o   In the **Keyboard Shortcuts** menu, you can choose from preset sets for different tasks (such as **Application Menus, Panel Menus,** or **Tools**).

2. **Assign Custom Shortcuts:**

   o   Select the function or tool you want to assign a shortcut to and click on it. Press the key combination you want to assign, and Photoshop will record it.

3. **Save the New Shortcuts:**

   o   Once you've made your changes, you can save the shortcut set for future use. This ensures you always have access to your custom hotkeys.

Using Modifier Keys for Quick Access:

In addition to custom shortcuts, you can use **modifier keys** like **Shift, Ctrl/Cmd, Alt/Option,** and **Spacebar** to temporarily access tools without changing the selected tool. For instance:

- **Hold Shift** while using a tool to constrain its movement (e.g., hold **Shift** while drawing a square with the Rectangle Tool).

- **Spacebar** temporarily switches to the **Hand Tool** for moving around the canvas.

By mastering these shortcuts and customizing your hotkeys, you can access tools and commands faster, reducing the time spent on repetitive tasks.

Project: Designing a Complex Multi-Layered Artwork

Now that we've covered how to optimize your workflow, let's apply these techniques to create a **complex multi-layered artwork**. In this project, you'll design a **dynamic, layered composition** using **advanced masking, batch processing, actions,** and **custom keyboard shortcuts**.

Step 1: Set Up the Document

1. **Create a New Document**:

   ○ Set up a large canvas (e.g., **3000 x 4000 px**) with a resolution of **300 dpi** for high-quality output.

2. **Organize Layers**:

   ○ Create folders for different sections of the design (e.g., **Background**, **Text**, **Graphics**, **Effects**) to keep things organized.

Step 2: Import and Mask Elements

1. **Import Images**:

   ○ Bring in your main elements, such as photos, icons, and vector graphics, using **File > Place Embedded**.

2. **Use Advanced Masking**:

   ○ Apply **advanced masking** techniques to isolate the subject from the background, using **channels** and **refine edge tools** for clean edges.

Step 3: Apply Batch Processing

1. **Batch Process Textures**:

   ○ Use **actions** to batch process textures or other repetitive tasks, such as applying a certain effect across multiple images.

2. **Optimize for Export**:

   ○ Set up **batch processing** to resize or optimize images for export to the web or print.

Step 4: Finalize with Custom Shortcuts

1. **Refine and Polish**:

   o Use **keyboard shortcuts** to quickly access tools like **Clone Stamp**, **Brush**, and **Transform** to refine your design.

2. **Export for Different Mediums**:

   o Use custom actions and **batch processing** to export your artwork in various formats for different platforms (e.g., **JPEG** for web, **TIFF** for print).

Optimizing Photoshop Settings for Performance and Efficiency

Photoshop includes a number of adjustable parameters that can drastically affect your performance. Whether you're editing high-resolution photographs, making complicated compositions, or running several processes, tweaking your settings right can greatly enhance speed and efficiency.

Understanding Photoshop's Performance Settings

The Performance options in Photoshop allow you to alter how the software uses your computer's resources, such as RAM, CPU, and scratch disks. Properly adjusting these parameters ensures that Photoshop operates smoothly, especially when working with huge files or complicated projects.

How to Adjust Photoshop's Performance Settings:

1. **Accessing Performance Settings**:

   o Go to **Edit > Preferences > Performance** (Windows) or **Photoshop > Preferences > Performance** (Mac). This section lets you control key performance settings in Photoshop.

2. **Allocate RAM**:

   o The more **RAM** Photoshop has access to, the better it will perform, especially for large files. In the **Performance** panel, you can set the **RAM Usage** slider to allow Photoshop to use more RAM.

- As a general guideline, allocate **70-80% of your computer's total RAM** to Photoshop. Be sure to leave some RAM for other programs, so your computer doesn't slow down.

3. **Scratch Disks**:

   - **Scratch disks** are hard drives that Photoshop uses when it runs out of RAM. The more space available on your scratch disk, the better Photoshop can perform.

   - If possible, use an **SSD** (Solid-State Drive) as your scratch disk, as it provides faster data access than traditional hard drives.

   - To set up or change your scratch disks, go to **Preferences > Scratch Disks** and select the drive with the most free space available.

4. **History States**:

   - Photoshop stores a history of your actions, allowing you to **undo** or **redo** changes. The **History States** setting determines how many steps Photoshop saves in its history.

   - Reducing the number of **History States** can help improve performance, especially when working with large files. A setting between **20 to 50 history states** is typically sufficient for most projects.

5. **Adjusting Cache Levels**:

   - Photoshop's **Cache Levels** setting controls how much data Photoshop keeps in memory for quick access. Increasing the cache levels helps improve performance when working with large files or complex edits.

   - For most users, a **Cache Level** of **4** or **6** provides a good balance between performance and file size. For extremely large images, you may want to increase the cache level to **8**.

6. **Graphics Processor Settings**:

   - Photoshop uses the **Graphics Processor Unit (GPU)** to accelerate tasks such as **rendering 3D objects** and **applying certain filters**.

- Enable **Use Graphics Processor** in the **Performance** settings and ensure that Photoshop is using your computer's **dedicated GPU** (if available). You can also tweak GPU-related settings for specific tasks under **Preferences > Performance > GPU Settings**.

7. **Disabling Features You Don't Use**:

   - If you don't use certain features like **3D rendering**, **animated brushes**, or **OpenGL** filters, consider disabling them to save system resources. This can be done in the **Performance** settings under **Advanced Settings**.

Additional Tips for Performance:

- **Close Unnecessary Files and Applications**: The more files and applications you have open, the more resources Photoshop needs to manage. Close unnecessary files and applications to improve Photoshop's performance.

- **Optimize Your Documents**: Large, high-resolution documents can bog down your system. If you're working on a large project, try working in **smaller sections** and then combining them later.

Working with External Hardware: Tablets, Graphics Cards, and Monitors

The appropriate hardware setup can substantially improve your workflow in Photoshop, whether you're a photographer, designer, or illustrator. From employing graphic tablets to exploiting the power of dedicated graphics cards and high-resolution displays, each piece of hardware plays a critical part in maximizing your Photoshop experience.

Using a Graphics Tablet for Precision

A graphics tablet (also known as a drawing tablet) is a useful tool for designers and artists who need to make precise, fluid movements in Photoshop. Whether you're drawing, painting, or retouching, a tablet delivers pressure sensitivity and control that a mouse cannot equal.

Choosing the Right Tablet:

1. **Wacom Tablets** are the most popular among Photoshop users, offering both professional-level performance and compatibility.

2. **Pressure Sensitivity** is important for tasks like drawing or painting, as it controls the size and opacity of the brush strokes. A tablet with **8192 levels of pressure sensitivity** will offer the best control.

Using the Tablet in Photoshop:

1. **Customize Your Brushes**: Many brushes in Photoshop have settings that are sensitive to pen pressure. Make sure that your tablet is configured to take advantage of **pressure sensitivity** when using brushes, allowing for dynamic strokes.

2. **Use Tablet Shortcuts**: Most graphic tablets come with programmable buttons that can be assigned to commonly used Photoshop tools. This will help speed up your workflow by allowing you to access tools with one click.

Optimizing Your Graphics Card for Photoshop

A **dedicated graphics card** is one of the most significant hardware upgrades you can make for Photoshop. Graphics cards (GPUs) are responsible for accelerating performance in tasks like **3D rendering, filter application**, and **image manipulation**.

Why is a GPU Important in Photoshop?

- **3D Rendering**: For artists working with 3D objects or textures, a powerful GPU is essential. Photoshop uses the GPU to accelerate **rendering** and **real-time display** of 3D models.

- **Acceleration for Filters**: Many of Photoshop's **filter effects**, such as **Oil Paint** and **Lens Blur**, can be accelerated by the GPU for faster performance.

How to Optimize Your GPU:

1. Ensure that **GPU acceleration** is turned on in the **Performance** tab of the **Preferences** settings.

2. Update your GPU drivers regularly to maintain compatibility with the latest features in Photoshop 2025.

Working with Monitors: The Importance of Display Resolution and Color Accuracy

Monitors are one of the most overlooked pieces of hardware in a Photoshop workflow. The **resolution** and **color accuracy** of your display directly impact how you perceive your designs and edits.

Choosing the Right Monitor:

1. **Resolution**: A higher resolution monitor allows you to work on larger canvases with more detail. If you frequently work with high-resolution images, opt for a **4K** or **5K** monitor.

2. **Color Accuracy**: Color-sensitive work, like **photo editing** and **graphic design**, requires a monitor that can display accurate colors. Look for a monitor with a high **color gamut** (such as **Adobe RGB** or **sRGB**).

Calibrating Your Monitor:

1. **Use a Hardware Calibration Tool**: Tools like the **X-Rite i1Display Pro** can help you calibrate your monitor to ensure that the colors you see are accurate.

2. **Adjust Photoshop's Color Settings**: In **Edit > Color Settings**, adjust the **working spaces** for RGB and CMYK to ensure Photoshop matches the color profile of your monitor.

Troubleshooting and Fixing Common Photoshop Problems

Despite being one of the most powerful creative tools, Photoshop can occasionally run into issues, especially with large files or complex workflows. Understanding common problems and how to troubleshoot them can save you time and frustration.

Common Photoshop Issues and Their Solutions:

1. **Photoshop Running Slowly**:

   ○ **Solution**: Adjust your **Performance Settings** (as discussed in Section 1), increase your **RAM allocation**, and ensure you have enough free space on your **scratch disk**. Closing other resource-heavy applications will also help.

2. **Photoshop Freezing or Crashing**:

   ○ **Solution**: Photoshop may freeze or crash if it runs out of memory. Try **resetting preferences** by holding **Ctrl + Alt + Shift** (Windows) or **Cmd + Option + Shift** (Mac) when launching Photoshop. If the issue persists, update Photoshop to the latest version or reinstall the program.

3. **Brush Lag:**

   ○ **Solution**: Brush lag can be caused by high **resolution settings** or large brush sizes. Try reducing the resolution of your document or decreasing the brush size. Ensure **GPU acceleration** is enabled in the **Performance** settings.

4. **Missing or Corrupted Files**:

   ○ **Solution**: If files are missing or corrupted, always keep a backup of your important projects. Use the **File Recovery** options within Photoshop to retrieve previous versions of your work.

Final Project: Creating an Efficient Photoshop Workflow from Start to Finish

Now that we've covered the key optimization techniques, it's time to apply them in a practical project. In this section, you'll design a **complex composition** using an efficient workflow, from file organization to using automation tools.

Step 1: Set Up the Workspace and Files

1. **Organize Your Files**:

   ○ Create a folder structure for your project. Label folders for **Images**, **Assets**, **Working Files**, and **Exports**. This organization will help you stay efficient and avoid confusion.

2. **Optimize Performance Settings**:

   ○ Adjust your **RAM allocation**, set up **scratch disks**, and tweak the **History States** and **Cache Levels** to optimize Photoshop for performance.

Step 2: Use Actions and Batch Processing

1. **Create Actions**:

   ○ Record an **action** to automatically apply edits such as **resizing images, applying filters**, or **adjusting brightness/contrast**.

2. **Batch Process**:

   ○ Use **Batch Processing** to apply the action to multiple images. This can be useful for resizing images for a website or applying a specific filter to a set of assets.

Step 3: Utilize External Hardware

1. **Use Your Graphics Tablet**:

   o Create detailed elements of your composition using the **graphics tablet** to draw or paint with **pressure-sensitive brushes**.

2. **Work with Your Monitor**:

   o Ensure that your monitor is calibrated correctly and adjust Photoshop's **color settings** to match your display's color profile for accurate design work.

Step 4: Finalize and Export the Composition

1. **Apply Finishing Touches**:

   o Use **layer styles**, **smart objects**, and **adjustment layers** to give your design a polished look. Double-check the organization of your layers to ensure everything is in place.

2. **Export Efficiently**:

   o Use **Save for Web** and **Batch Processing** to export your assets in different formats for use on websites, in print, or in apps.

In this chapter, we've discussed how to improve your Photoshop experience to maximize both speed and creativity. From altering performance settings and working with external devices to diagnosing common issues, we've covered a number of tools and approaches to streamline your process. By using these adjustments, you can substantially enhance your Photoshop productivity and free up more time for the creative chores you enjoy.

As you move forward, continue to experiment with the strategies described here, such as automating jobs with actions, organizing your files for ease of access, and employing the latest technology to increase your performance.

An effective Photoshop workflow is vital for delivering high-quality work in a timely way, and by implementing these techniques, you can unlock the full potential of Photoshop 2025.

Chapter 13

Final Tips and Tricks for Enhancing Your Photoshop Experience

Adobe Photoshop has established itself as the top software for creative professionals. Whether you're editing photographs, making graphics, or producing digital artwork, Photoshop offers a broad toolset that allows you to bring your creative vision to life. However, learning Photoshop's functionality goes beyond comprehending its basic tools. The key to becoming fully proficient is learning how to optimize your workflow, which involves mastering vital keyboard shortcuts, comprehending important Photoshop keywords, and having access to tools like FAQs for addressing frequent issues.

with this Appendix, we'll give a complete collection of materials to help you enhance your workflow and become more productive with Photoshop 2025. From a list of keyboard shortcuts that will substantially shorten your time on jobs to a glossary of important Photoshop phrases to clear up any confusion, and lastly, solutions to some of the most often asked issues by Photoshop users.

By the end of this appendix, you will be able to work faster, fix common issues, and better understand the entire variety of features that Photoshop 2025 has to offer.

Photoshop 2025 Keyboard Shortcuts

The Photoshop Keyboard Shortcuts are designed to speed up your productivity, allowing you to access tools and perform tasks with a single key combination. Whether you're a seasoned Photoshop professional or just starting out, learning the appropriate shortcuts will help you navigate the software faster and boost your efficiency.

Here is a comprehensive list of essential **keyboard shortcuts** in **Photoshop 2025**:

Basic Shortcuts:

- **Ctrl + N (Windows) / Cmd + N (Mac)**: New Document

- **Ctrl + O (Windows) / Cmd + O (Mac)**: Open File

- **Ctrl + S (Windows) / Cmd + S (Mac)**: Save File

- **Ctrl + Shift + S (Windows) / Cmd + Shift + S (Mac)**: Save As

- **Ctrl + P (Windows) / Cmd + P (Mac)**: Print

- **Ctrl + Q (Windows) / Cmd + Q (Mac)**: Quit Photoshop

- **Ctrl + Z (Windows) / Cmd + Z (Mac)**: Undo/Redo (Step Forward or Step Backward in the history)

Tool Shortcuts:

- **V**: Move Tool

- **M**: Marquee Tool (Rectangle, Elliptical)

- **L**: Lasso Tool

- **W**: Magic Wand Tool

- **C**: Crop Tool

- **B**: Brush Tool

- **E**: Eraser Tool

- **G**: Gradient Tool

- **T**: Type Tool

- **P**: Pen Tool

- **I**: Eyedropper Tool

- **H**: Hand Tool (for moving the canvas)

- **Z**: Zoom Tool

- **U**: Shape Tool

- **R**: Rotate View Tool

Selection and Editing Shortcuts:

- **Ctrl + A (Windows) / Cmd + A (Mac):** Select All

- **Ctrl + D (Windows) / Cmd + D (Mac):** Deselect Selection

- **Ctrl + Shift + I (Windows) / Cmd + Shift + I (Mac):** Inverse Selection

- **Ctrl + Shift + N (Windows) / Cmd + Shift + N (Mac):** New Layer

- **Ctrl + J (Windows) / Cmd + J (Mac):** Duplicate Layer

- **Ctrl + E (Windows) / Cmd + E (Mac):** Merge Layers

- **Ctrl + G (Windows) / Cmd + G (Mac):** Group Layers

- **Ctrl + T (Windows) / Cmd + T (Mac):** Free Transform

- **Ctrl + Shift + T (Windows) / Cmd + Shift + T (Mac):** Repeat Transformation

Layer Management Shortcuts:

- **Ctrl + Shift + N (Windows) / Cmd + Shift + N (Mac):** Create New Layer

- **Ctrl + G (Windows) / Cmd + G (Mac):** Group Layers

- **Ctrl + Shift + G (Windows) / Cmd + Shift + G (Mac):** Ungroup Layers

- **Alt + Ctrl + G (Windows) / Option + Cmd + G (Mac):** Create Clipping Mask

- **Ctrl + Alt + Shift + N (Windows) / Cmd + Option + Shift + N (Mac):** Create New Layer without Dialog Box

Adjustment Shortcuts:

- **Ctrl + L (Windows) / Cmd + L (Mac):** Levels

- **Ctrl + M (Windows) / Cmd + M (Mac):** Curves

- **Ctrl + U (Windows) / Cmd + U (Mac):** Hue/Saturation

- **Ctrl + Shift + L (Windows) / Cmd + Shift + L (Mac)**: Auto Tone

- **Ctrl + Shift + B (Windows) / Cmd + Shift + B (Mac)**: Auto Color

- **Ctrl + Alt + I (Windows) / Cmd + Option + I (Mac)**: Image Size

Navigation Shortcuts:

- **Spacebar**: Temporarily switch to Hand Tool

- **Ctrl + + (Windows) / Cmd + + (Mac)**: Zoom In

- **Ctrl + - (Windows) / Cmd + - (Mac)**: Zoom Out

- **Ctrl + 0 (Windows) / Cmd + 0 (Mac)**: Fit to Screen

- **Ctrl + 1 (Windows) / Cmd + 1 (Mac)**: Actual Pixels (100% zoom)

- **Ctrl + Alt + 0 (Windows) / Cmd + Option + 0 (Mac)**: Fit on Screen (without borders)

Glossary of Key Photoshop Terms

Understanding key Photoshop terminology is essential for mastering the software and making the most out of its features. Below is a glossary of important terms that will help you comprehend the language of Photoshop and guide your creative workflow.

A:

- **Adjustment Layer**: A non-destructive layer that allows you to apply effects like brightness, contrast, and color adjustments to an image without altering the original image layer.

- **Alpha Channel**: A grayscale image used to store selections, transparency, or layer masks. It can be saved separately and used as a mask for images.

B:

- **Bitmap**: A type of image made up of a grid of individual pixels, commonly used for photographs or detailed designs.

- **Brush Tool**: A tool used for painting, drawing, and applying textures. Brushes in Photoshop come in a variety of shapes and sizes, and they can be customized for different effects.

C:

- **Clone Stamp Tool**: A tool that allows you to copy a selected area of an image and paint it over another area, useful for retouching or duplicating parts of an image.

- **Channels**: Separate color components in an image, such as Red, Green, and Blue for RGB images or Cyan, Magenta, Yellow, and Black for CMYK images.

- **Clipping Mask**: A way of masking layers so that one layer only affects the area of the layer below it. The clipping mask is created by placing a layer above the base layer, and the top layer is clipped to the shape of the lower layer.

D:

- **Depth of Field**: The distance between the nearest and farthest objects in a photo that appears in focus.

- **Dodge and Burn**: Tools used to lighten (dodge) or darken (burn) specific areas of an image, commonly used in photo retouching.

E:

- **Exposure**: The amount of light that reaches the camera sensor or film, affecting the brightness and contrast of an image.

- **Eyedropper Tool**: A tool used to sample colors from an image, allowing you to select colors accurately for painting or design purposes.

F:

- **Filters**: Predefined effects applied to an image to modify its appearance, such as blurring, sharpening, or distorting.

- **Flattener**: The process of merging multiple layers into one layer in order to reduce file size.

G:

- **Gradient**: A gradual transition from one color to another, often used for background fills or subtle transitions in an image.

- **Grayscale**: An image mode consisting of shades of gray, typically used for black-and-white photos or designs.

H:

- **Histogram**: A graphical representation of the tonal values in an image, used to evaluate the exposure and contrast of the image.

- **Hue**: The color or shade of an object or image, represented in the color wheel.

L:

- **Layers**: Different levels of content in a Photoshop file, allowing for non-destructive editing. Layers can be text, images, shapes, and more.

- **Lens Blur**: A filter that simulates the appearance of a blurry image from the effect of a camera lens.

M:

- **Mask**: A tool used for hiding or revealing parts of a layer non-destructively, used to create transitions, layer effects, or remove unwanted elements.

- **Merge**: The process of combining multiple layers into one, used to consolidate the design or image.

P:

- **Pen Tool**: A tool used to create precise paths, selections, and shapes by placing anchor points and curves.

- **Pixel**: The smallest unit of an image, typically square-shaped, and used to build up an image on screen.

Frequently Asked Questions (FAQ)

Here are some of the most frequently asked questions about Photoshop 2025, along with detailed answers to help resolve any confusion you may encounter while using the software.

Q1: How Can I Speed Up Photoshop When Working with Large Files?

A1: Working with large files can significantly slow down Photoshop. To speed up your performance, try the following:

- **Increase RAM allocation**: Go to **Preferences > Performance** and allocate more memory to Photoshop.

- **Use an SSD for scratch disks**: Set up **scratch disks** on an SSD to ensure faster data access.

- **Disable unnecessary layers**: Temporarily hide layers that you're not working with to reduce the load on Photoshop.

- **Reduce History States**: Lower the number of history states in **Preferences > Performance** to reduce the memory usage.

Q2: How Do I Create a Custom Brush in Photoshop?

A2: Creating a custom brush in Photoshop is simple:

1. Create an image or shape that you want to turn into a brush (e.g., a texture or design).

2. Select the image and go to **Edit > Define Brush Preset**.

3. Name your brush and click **OK**. You can now select the brush tool and use your custom brush.

Q3: Can I Use Photoshop for 3D Design?

A3: Yes, Photoshop 2025 includes a variety of 3D features. You can create 3D objects, apply textures, and even render 3D models within Photoshop. To start, go to **3D > New 3D Layer from Selected Path** to create 3D objects from paths or shapes.

Q4: Why Is My Photoshop Lagging or Freezing?

A4: Photoshop may lag or freeze for a variety of reasons, including insufficient RAM or corrupted preferences. Try the following to resolve the issue:

- **Clear your cache**: Go to **Preferences > Performance** and clear the cache to free up memory.

- **Reset preferences**: Hold **Ctrl + Alt + Shift** (Windows) or **Cmd + Option + Shift** (Mac) while launching Photoshop to reset preferences.

- **Update Photoshop**: Make sure you are using the latest version of Photoshop for optimal performance.

Q5: How Do I Export My Photoshop Files for Web Use?

A5: To export files optimized for the web, go to **File > Export > Save for Web (Legacy)**. Choose the appropriate format (JPEG, PNG, GIF) and adjust the quality, resolution, and file size to ensure fast loading times without compromising image quality.

This Appendix has given you crucial resources to assist in maximizing your Photoshop experience. From keyboard shortcuts and a full vocabulary of Photoshop jargon to troubleshooting common issues and answering commonly asked questions, this area will serve as a vital reference for enhancing your efficiency and resolving any challenges you may find with Photoshop 2025.

By learning these tools and resources, you can boldly take your creative work to new heights while working more efficiently in Photoshop.

Conclusion

As you close this book and move into the realm of Adobe Photoshop 2025, you are now armed with the knowledge and skills to raise your creative process to new heights. From the basics of design to the sophisticated techniques that push the boundaries of digital artistry, Photoshop is not simply a tool—it's a gateway to endless creative possibilities.

Through learning keyboard shortcuts, sophisticated masking, workflow optimization, and harnessing Photoshop's tremendous capabilities, you have learned how to optimize your process, boost your productivity, and finally unlock your full creative potential. Photoshop is a dynamic platform, giving more than simply photo editing; it's a canvas for artistic expression, a workshop for digital creations, and a versatile tool for designers, photographers, illustrators, and digital artists of all types.

Whether you're designing for the web, constructing captivating photo compositions, or exploring with 3D elements, filters, and custom brushes, Photoshop 2025 is an amazing resource that empowers you to bring your ideas to life with precision, clarity, and efficiency. The secret to success in mastering Photoshop isn't just about learning how to utilize its tools—it's about understanding how to use them in harmony to boost your workflow, increase your productivity, and allow your creative ideas to blossom without limits.

The creative road is never a straight path, but with Photoshop as your buddy, you have the liberty to experiment, fail, and refine your art until every creation is an expression of your vision and skill.

As you continue to explore and invent with Photoshop 2025, remember that the actual strength of this software rests in your ability to push beyond the bounds of your imagination. Let this guidance serve as a foundation, and always strive to learn, adapt, and progress as an artist in the digital age. The options are boundless, and with Photoshop in your hands, there are no restrictions to what you may make.

Go Forth And Create, And May Your Work Reflect The Passion, Expertise, And Originality That You Bring To Every Project. The World Of Digital Art Is Waiting For Your Next Masterpiece.